Practical Property Management

BY DAVE RAVINDRA

Order this book online at www.trafford.com
or email orders@trafford.com

Most Trafford titles are also available at major online book retailers.

© Copyright 2010 Dave Ravindra.
All rights reserved. No part of this publication may be reproduced, stored in a retrieval system, or transmitted, in any form or by any means, electronic, mechanical, photocopying, recording, or otherwise, without the written prior permission of the author.

Printed in Victoria, BC, Canada.

ISBN: 978-1-4269-1652-6 (sc)

Our mission is to efficiently provide the world's finest, most comprehensive book publishing service, enabling every author to experience success. To find out how to publish your book, your way, and have it available worldwide, visit us online at www.trafford.com

Trafford rev. 2/18/2010

Trafford PUBLISHING   www.trafford.com

North America & international
toll-free: 1 888 232 4444 (USA & Canada)
phone: 250 383 6864 ♦ fax: 812 355 4082

The material herein are provided with the understanding that the author, the company, and/or publisher are NOT engaged in rendering legal, investment, and/or tax advice, tax services, or accounting, as they may be related to this publication.

Questions regarding the specific accounting, legal, investment and/or tax needs of any reader should be addressed to his/her own professional advisor.

Canadian Real Estate Investment Group (CANREIG), the author, editor(s), its agent and assigns, specifically disclaim any liability, loss or risk personal or otherwise incurred as a consequence directly or indirectly of the use and/or application of these techniques and/or materials provided herein. The forms and examples are provided for educational purposes only. These forms and examples may not be appropriate for use in all provinces, therefore you should request your professional advisor to review these or any forms you plan on using for any purpose.

NO PART OF THIS BOOK MAY BE REPRODUCED IN ANY FORM, BY ANY MEANS, WITHOUT THE WRITTEN PERMISSION FROM THE AUTHOR.

© 2010 Canadian Real Estate Investment Group

Foreword:

Ever since I met Dave over nine years ago, I have been intrigued by his knowledge in the real world of real estate investing. He is a charismatic man that has a wealth of experience that he's not afraid to share. I appreciate his no fluff, no nonsense approach to teaching people on how to become incredibly successful in real estate investing. He's a true go-getter who loves what he does, and a great teacher. Being personally mentored by him over the years, I have grown in both knowledge and wealth. Dave, along with his network of professionals, helped me purchase my first investment property many years ago. But it didn't stop there. He continued to encourage action and results, and with that, I am very happy with what I've amassed, and continue to grow and expand my real estate portfolio. To this I owe him a big Thank You!

This book is a great, hands-on approach to learning how to properly manage properties. Dave definitely has experience in all aspects of real estate and I feel that no where else can you get this type of direct, applicable information than from him.

Sincerely,

Wendy Singh

Preface:

This book has been in the works for many years. It was started because I was constantly being asked the same questions about how to manage properties. Having over 20 years of experience in real estate, I've made many mistakes, learned from these mistakes and have a strong desire to teach others from my experience so they don't have to make the same mistakes, achieving their real estate goals more efficiently. I thoroughly enjoy seeking out lucrative opportunities; regardless of how near or far they are from where I live. It's only natural that I've acquired contacts and the know how on how to manage properties and projects from a distance, and I'll share what I've learned with you throughout this book.

I want to thank many of the CANREIG Members for encouraging me to complete this book. It wasn't a priority at first, but as CANREIG continued to grow, the urgency in getting the right information into the right people's hands was immense.

Many people assisted in gathering the research for this book. I would personally like to acknowledge and thank Ametra Dave for her persistence and due diligence on the various tenancy laws when it comes to property management. In addition, Deen Bissessar, with his background as a Realtor, assisted in rules regarding leases. Rita Bahadur needs to be credited for her ongoing support. As well, I would like to acknowledge Wendy Singh for her attention to detail, finessing and input for putting together this book.

I anticipate that this book will be a great resource for many Canadian real estate investors. It took me many years to learn the hard way, but by sharing my knowledge via this book, I hope it will shave off many years of your own personal experience and you can benefit from not making the mistakes I did.

Sincerely,

Dave Ravindra

(Please Note: To facilitate the reading of this document, he, him, himself and his are used as generic terms, and are not used in a gender-specific sense.)

Contents

INTRODUCTION xiii

Chapter 1:
PROPERTY MANAGEMENT 1
- ❑ TYPES OF PROPERTY MANAGEMENT 1
    - Self-Management 2
    - Resident Management 2
    - Professional Management 3
- ❑ EMPLOYMENT APPLICATION FOR PROPERTY MANAGER 5

Chapter 2:
YOUR TENANTS 9
- ❑ WHO ARE YOUR TENANTS? 9
- ❑ ADVERTISING FOR TENANTS 11
    - Types Of Advertisements 12
    - How To Design An Advertisement 18
    - Helpful Abbreviations 21
    - The Telephone And The Answering Machine 22
    - What To Say To Potential Tenants On The Phone 25
    - Screening Criteria 27
    - Be Aware Of These Potential Tenants 28
- ❑ SCHEDULING AN APPOINTMENT TO SEE THE RENTAL PROPERTY 31
    - How To Cut Down On No-Shows 31
    - Showing The Property To Potential Tenants 32
    - Saying Yes To A Potential Tenant 32
    - Saying No To A Potential Tenant 32
- ❑ RENTAL APPLICATIONS 33
- ❑ EMPLOYMENT VERIFICATION INQUIRY LETTER 41
- ❑ CREDIT CHECK INQUIRY LETTER 43
- ❑ LANDLORD/TENANT UNIT INSPECTION 45
- ❑ LANDLORD/TENANT INVENTORY FOR FURNISHED UNITS 50

Chapter 3:
LEASES 55
- ❑ THE LEASE DOCUMENT 55
  - The Consequences Of A Written Document 56
- ❑ TYPES OF LEASES 57
  - Gross Lease 57
  - Net Lease 57
  - Single-Net Lease 58
  - Net-Net Lease 58
  - Net-Net-Net Lease 58
  - Percentage Lease 58
- ❑ THE ELEMENTS OF A VALID LEASE 59
  - The Contracting Parties 59
  - Obtaining A Spouse's Signature 62
  - The Depiction Of The Leased Premises 62
  - Supporting The Agreement 62
  - The Use Of The Premises 63
  - Expiration Dates 64
  - The Rights And Obligations Of The Parties 64
- ❑ COVENANTS (PLEDGES OR PROMISES) 64
  - Regular Or Standard Lease Covenants 65
- ❑ CONTENTS OF A LEASE 76
- ❑ SPECIAL COVENANTS 81
- ❑ TERMINATION OF TENANCY AGREEMENT 85
- ❑ SPECIAL CLAUSES 85
  - For Office Buildings (Commercial) 85
  - For Retail And Shopping Centres 86
- ❑ SAMPLE LEASE AGREEMENTS 89
  - Residential Lease 90
  - Lease Renewal Agreement 93
  - Agreement To Terminate a Tenancy 94

Chapter 4:
PROPERTY MAINTENANCE 95
- ❑ MAINTAINING YOUR RENTAL PROPERTY 95
  - Initial Considerations 96
- ❑ ASPECTS OF A RENTAL PROPERTY 98
  - The Grounds 98
  - Exterior Maintenance 102

- Interior Common Areas 105
- Inside The Rental Unit 108
- ❑ WORKING WITH INDEPENDENT CONTRACTORS 110
  - Finding Your Subcontractors 111
- ❑ THE CONTRACTOR'S PAPERWORK 111
  - Certificates Of Insurance 112
  - Getting Bids 112
  - Letting Contractors Into The Rental Units 113
  - Preparing For Night Calls 113
- ❑ A SHORT CONCLUSION 113

Chapter 5:
PROPERTY MANAGEMENT & THE LAW 115
- ❑ MUNICIPAL LEGISLATION 115
- ❑ PROVINCIAL LEGISLATION 115
- ❑ THE LANDLORD AND TENANT ACT OF ONTARIO 116
- ❑ SUMMARY OF PART IV OF THE ACT 117
  - Who Is Affected? 119
  - What Is A Residential Dwelling? 119
  - Tenancy Agreements 119
  - Security Deposits 120
  - Key Money 120
  - Privacy And Access 121
  - Repairs And Maintenance 121
  - Subletting 122
  - Mobile Homes 123
  - Rent Increases 123
  - Ending A Tenancy 124
  - Notice Of Termination 124
- ❑ A TENANT'S RIGHTS AND LEGAL REMEDIES 130
- ❑ A LANDLORD'S RIGHTS AND LEGAL REMEDIES 131
  - Evictions 131
  - Vital Services 131
- ❑ TENANT SECURITY 132
- ❑ POSTING THE ACT 132
- ❑ OFFENCES AND PENALTIES 132
- ❑ DWELLINGS NOT COVERED BY THE ACT 133

CONCLUSION 135
GLOSSARY 137

Introduction

Property management consists not only of cosmetic chores (grounds keeping, garbage removal, lawn/driveway care) and maintenance tasks, but also administrative duties such as collecting rents, dealing with tenant concerns, selecting tenants, and paying bills. There are various means that you can use to outsource property management tasks, however this will depend on your budget and what skills you have to do the work yourself.

Over the next five chapters you will be exposed to the various types of property management, how to work with tenants, how to inspect a property (including checklists), working with leases and understanding how a lease protects both you and the tenant, maintaining property and legislation relating to property management.

Chapter 1:
Property Management

As mentioned in the introduction, property management involves much more than just finding tenants and working with tenant issues. It may include labour around the property grounds, marketing and more. In order to understand the various extents of property management, let's visit how to determine what type of property management is needed in different scenarios.

TYPES OF PROPERTY MANAGEMENT

There are three main types of property management. The determining factors of which type to choose include:

- Whether property management appeals to you
- What sort of management experience you have
- The size and type of property
- The size and number of other investments you have to look after
- The number of tenants
- The amount of time you have to devote to managing property

Combinations of the following categories are not uncommon. Determine what would be most practical and affordable for you.

SELF-MANAGEMENT

It is up to you how involved you want to be in managing the real estate you have invested in. One option is to be fairly involved in the operation and/or maintenance of your property or properties – this is known as self-management.

This arrangement may be more practical and cost-efficient than delegating the managerial duties to others, when dealing with small revenue properties (a single-family house or duplex).

This does not necessarily mean you would be responsible for grounds keeping, such as grass cutting, garbage removal, driveway maintenance, etc. However, it does mean that either you or someone on your behalf (either a company under contract, or perhaps even the residents themselves) would be involved in overseeing these sorts of operations, among others.

If you do choose to manage or assist in managing property yourself, make sure you can make the requisite time available to do so. It is possible to work a full-time job and manage property in your free time, but this may take advanced time-management skills that you would have to build up over time.

If you are hoping to involve tenants in the general upkeep of the property, be prepared to offer them some sort of compensation for their labour. Be sure to discuss these arrangements when they initially move in.

RESIDENT MANAGEMENT

Resident management consists of one or more individuals working for the owner to look after his/her property (or properties).

The resident manager resides in one of the units in the property – therefore, this arrangement is commonly applied to condominiums, multi-unit dwellings and apartments – properties with many units – otherwise it might not be financially feasible to employ someone.

This can be a part-time or full-time position, with a salary or rent-free tenancy in exchange for services. A tenant already residing in the building could possibly be considered for employment, rather than hiring someone new. Often, a husband-and-wife management team makes for a good set-up.

A successful resident property manager should be:

- reliable and diligent in terms of the actual work concerned
- competent and able to complete necessary tasks
- amiable, with strong communication skills
- organized, using time efficiently
- familiar with the service industry in some relevant way
- takes pleasure in work well done and the labour involved
- has prior experience with maintenance and upkeep

The Resident Manager's Duties

The resident manager's responsibilities can fluctuate from property to property, but here is a general list of common functions:

- grounds keeping
- collection of rents and making deposits
- showing unoccupied units to prospective tenants
- assessing and making decisions about prospective tenants
- keeping records
- general maintenance and repairs
- informing you of any issues or problems that may come up

In some ways, you have delegated the owner's responsibilities to the resident manager. Therefore, it is important to entrust these tasks only to someone who you can depend on. Be careful in your selection of the resident manager, and be sure to make a very thorough check of all references.

PROFESSIONAL MANAGEMENT

Many owners of several single-family dwellings, apartment buildings over 12 units, and absentee owners utilize a professional management company to look after their building(s). Professional management companies are usually rather experienced at residential management and have many procedures that increase the efficiency of management.

Benefits of their service could include:

- computerized management, bookkeeping and accounting

- systems
- experienced staff
- knowledgeable, vigilant selection of and contracting out to trades people to do repair or service, subject to a limit beyond which any costs would require your permission
- selecting tenants, showing units, negotiating leases
- monitoring possible problems with tenants and evicting if necessary
- collecting rents
- paying all bills and mortgage payments on your behalf

An advantage of utilizing a professional management company is that it guarantees a high level of maintenance. The company will provide descriptions of what you expect done in writing, and include them in the management contract.

Fees for professional management companies can vary from 2% to 5% of the property's monthly revenue. The more the professional management company does for you, the more they will charge for the additional services.

Be sure to do comprehensive research on the company. Request references from other property-owning clients. Perhaps you can arrange to take a look at one of the properties currently being managed by the company.

You can find professional property managers in the Yellow Pages™ or online using www.YellowPages.ca™ under "Property Management." Additionally, you can search online via typing in the search words Property Management and your city or area. Look for the designation CPM that means Certified Property Manager. It denotes a high level of certification awarded by the Real Estate Institute of Canada.

The following pages include an example of an Employment Application Form that can be used when screening Property Managers.

EMPLOYMENT APPLICATION FOR PROPERTY MANAGER AND RELATED POSITIONS

Applicant's Name: _____

Street Address: _____

City: _____ Province: _____ Postal Code: _____

Work Phone: _____ Alternate Phone: _____

S.I.N. # _____

Driver's Licence # _____

Position Desired: _____

Desire Housing? Yes   No

CURRENT EMPLOYER

Employer's Name: _____

Employer's Address: _____

Employer's Phone: _____

Date of Employment: _____ to _____

What is/was your salary? _____

Responsibilities: _____
_____

Reason for leaving (if applicable): _____

Sample Employment Application Form for Property Managers

PREVIOUS EMPLOYERS

Employer's Name: _____

Employer's Address: _____

Employer's Phone: _____

Date of Employment: _____ to _____

What is/was your salary? _____

Responsibilities: _____

_____

Reason for leaving: _____

SKILLS
Circle either "yes" or "no" to each of the following:

Can you make minor plumbing repairs?	Yes	No
Can you make minor electrical repairs?	Yes	No
Can you do any painting?	Yes	No
Can you do any plastering?	Yes	No
Are you familiar with air conditioning systems?	Yes	No
Are you familiar with furnace operation?	Yes	No
Are you familiar with water heating systems?	Yes	No
Do you hold a D.C. Engineering license?	Yes	No
Are you familiar with pool maintenance?	Yes	No

EDUCATION

Name of School	Location (City, Province, Country)	Start Date	End Date	Degrees/ Diplomas Achieved

Sample Employment Application Form for Property Managers

Specific Training and Special Skills:
_____
_____
_____

Membership in technical or professional societies:
_____
_____

PERSONAL REFERENCES

Name: _____ Relationship: _____

Phone: _____

Name: _____ Relationship: _____

Phone: _____

EMERGENCY CONTACT

Name: _____ Relationship: _____

Phone: _____

Applicant Signature: _____ Date: _____

Sample Employment Application Form for Property Managers

THIS SPACE IS NOT TO BE FILLED BY THE APPLICANT

Interviewed by _____   Date _____

Remarks: _____

_____

Starting Date: _____   Salary or Rate: _____

OK To Hire: Yes   No
    If no, state reason: _____

Approved by (signature required): _____

Sample Employment Application Form for Property Managers

Chapter 2:

Your Tenants

WHO ARE YOUR TENANTS?

Perhaps the most important thing you can do to help ensure smooth property management is to make sure that you select responsible and considerate tenants – ones will who get along reasonably well with you, and with each other, if applicable.

One thing to keep in mind is that people do not necessarily choose to rent and to live with others. They cannot afford to buy a house or an apartment of their own, because they choose, however, to spend their money on things other than housing. Some may be putting aside money to pay for university or college tuition, go on a trip, or be able to afford a house or a condominium somewhere down the road. Others have to travel a lot for their jobs and because they aren't going to be home that often, prefer to keep housing costs low.

Money aside, some singles would rather live in a house than an apartment. They want to be able to go downstairs to use a washer and dryer, instead of going out to use the pay machines in a laundromat. Many of these tenants want a private backyard where they can get a suntan or grow their own vegetables.

Although most singles value their privacy, most also like to have people around for a little companionship and additional security. Many potential renters come from families with several siblings. Others spent some time in university or college dormitories or have lived in group houses during their school days.

Regardless of their personal preferences, all tenants want to have some control over whom they are going to be living with. Keep this in mind if you are choosing individual tenants. Individuals will desire to live with other tenants who have lifestyles that are compatible with their own.

Those who value neatness probably won't want to live with others who let the dishes stack up for days. Individuals who like a quiet lifestyle won't want to remain in a household where another tenant plays loud music most of the day. Many non-smokers do not want to be around smokers.

If you're going to be taking on tenants who are interested in your property as a group, then odds are they have already considered the fact that, the more their respective lifestyles can work together, the better the living situation will be.

If you're going to be taking on individual tenants, keep in mind that the first tenant you select is going to be critical to the formation of the household, since he is going to set the tone for the rest of the tenants who will follow. Indeed, that first individual is going to be instrumental in helping you select your other tenants.

It will be prudent for you to decide which characteristics you desire in your first tenant. You should then devise a strategy to find such a person. Obviously, you will want someone responsible, considerate, who will keep the house clean and, ideally, will be able to make simple repairs.

Unfortunately, the above criteria can be subjective, and difficult to discern easily. How can you really know, in a short meeting, if someone is truly responsible or considerate or handy? When you look for a tenant, you have to stick with objective criteria.

Age and sex are two very objective criteria. They also happen to be important criteria to most tenants who want to share a house with others. Many people who want to rent a shared house have very definite preferences about the age and sex of their housemates.

A person of 35 may not want an 18-year-old housemate, and vice versa. Many people also distinctly want to live with someone of the same sex, while others distinctly prefer a co-ed house.

One interesting thing to note is that some landlords find that when you run an advertisement which reads "male/female to share a house," three-quarters of your callers will be male. So, in advertising for male/

female, it may mean you will have fewer potential female tenants contacting you about renting.

Some landlords have also found that putting out advertisements which specify the type of person you are looking for, will get more responses than vaguely worded ads which imply that you'll take anyone as a tenant. In this respect, it is crucial to determine what criteria you will be placing in your advertisement, and what additional criteria you will use for screening once someone phones.

As mentioned, two of the criteria you may want to put into the ad are age and sex. A third critical criterion is the ability to pay the rent – you should state how much rent you are asking. In addition, you may want to include in your ad such screening devices as "non-smoker preferred" or "no pets, please," but these are not as critical. Once someone phones, you can screen for these traits.

Remember that the area in which your property is located and the type of dwelling it is will have a significant bearing in determining the types of tenants you will attract. This is another reason why it's smart to consider the type of tenants you prefer before placing your ad, and if possible, before purchasing your income property.

In most circumstances, children and young people tend to cause the most wear on a building. Be prepared for this if you decide to take in families with children. Perhaps the "safest" type of tenant is the older, working couple.

It is also useful to note that furnished apartments will attract more tenants who prefer a shorter rental period, as opposed to unfurnished apartments, which attract longer rentals. The same is said for one-bedroom apartments.

How and where you advertise will also have a bearing on the sorts of tenants who will be attracted. The readership of different newspapers, for example, may vary with factors such as lifestyle and income. We'll now take a look next at the various forms of advertisements a landlord can place.

ADVERTISING FOR TENANTS

How do you attract the right tenants? You advertise. A rental property in search of a tenant is a product you have to market just like any other product. You are competing against every other landlord out there with a property to rent, trying to attract desirable tenants. It helps to be somewhat aggressive and to get out there and let those tenants know what you have to offer.

First, you can make your rents attractive by pricing them about $25 below comparable rents for the area. To find out what the average rents are for the area, check these sources:

- local realtors
- newspaper ads
- rental agencies
- online rental and classified sites
- other relevant sources

If you're serious enough about property management to take on the landlording duties, then you will hopefully not have a problem doing the necessary research in order to figure out what you should charge. You should also have a good idea of the vacancy rate for your area and for properties similar to yours. Hopefully the average rent you could charge along with the low vacancy rate were criteria you considered when purchasing the property in the first place.

Equipped with this information, you should be able to construct an ad campaign that will get the house rented with minimal fuss and effort. If you have a strong landlord's market, a simple newspaper ad may be enough to keep your phone ringing off the hook. If it isn't, you may have to work at it a little.

TYPES OF ADVERTISEMENTS

Once you've figured out the tenant selection criteria you wish to employ, you next have to develop a strategy to find the people you want.

Examine your property and its geographic surroundings carefully. Is it a small house near a university? If so, you may think about advertising at the school, if that fits into your strategy. Students may be more likely to want to live in a small place.

Is the property near an army base? Then you may want to advertise there. Look at the surrounding area and examine it carefully – there may be a perfect venue where you can advertise for the sorts of tenants you desire to have.

There are a variety of forms of advertising that you can employ for your property:

- neighbours, friends, and colleagues
- current tenants
- public roommate-referral agencies
- private roommate-referral agencies
- organizational housing offices
- notices on bulletin boards
- signs
- real estate brokers
- newspaper and online classifieds

Let's look at each category in detail.

Neighbourhoods, Friends & Colleagues

If your neighbours, friends and colleagues know that you have a rental property, they can often be helpful in making referrals.

The chief advantage to this method, besides being free, is that your friends are likely to have acquaintances of a better calibre than you might find through a newspaper ad, and will in effect have done some of your screening for you.

The chief disadvantage to this method (and why you would never want to solely rely on it) is that your friends will probably have a very limited number of acquaintances who want to share a house. Such referrals will also occur sporadically, often at times when all of your rental properties are full.

Current Tenants

If you already have some tenants, they can be a valuable source of tenant referrals. They may have friends similar to themselves who are in need of a rental property. If your tenants are pleased with your management, they will be happy to let their friends know where they can get good housing at a fair price.

However, you won't be able to reach a very broad audience through your tenants and some referrals may be made when you don't have a vacancy.

Public Roommate – Referral Agencies

Some communities have publicly-funded programs to match house owners with tenants. There is usually little or no charge for utilizing the program.

In some areas, this service is limited to owners who want to share their own homes with renters, and investors are excluded. Other publicly funded programs work with owners of investment houses.

It is important to note that the target clientele of the publicly funded roommate-referral agencies may be senior citizens, the handicapped, the emotionally disturbed, and lower-income residents. They may or may not fit comfortably into your household as tenants.

If you are interested in this program, phone your local government office. Find out what programs, if any, exist in your area, and ask whether the office is willing to work with you.

Private Roommate – Referral Agencies

Private roommate-referral agencies usually charge a flat fee, whether or not they find an acceptable tenant for you. The fee may range from $25 to $50, or more. The quality of the service will most likely vary from one agency to another.

The top agencies do the most pre-screening. They will give you a questionnaire and ask you to specify which characteristics you prefer your tenants to have. Personnel from some agencies will even visit your rental house in order to describe it accurately to potential tenants.

You can find the names of private roommate-referral agencies in the Yellow Pages™, in the classified section of your newspaper, or online. Before you engage an agency's services, you may want to check with people who have used the agency to find out if they were satisfied.

Your local Better Business Bureau can be a useful source of information to find out if any complaints have been lodged against the firm you plan to work with.

If your time is extremely limited, you may want to use the services of a private roommate-referral agency. Otherwise, it may be more beneficial for you to recruit tenants yourself.

For one thing, the agency's clientele is likely to be relatively limited, since most prospective tenants prefer to search on their own. For another, an agency is an intermediary – though what you ideally want is to have immediate, direct contact with potential tenants.

Direct contact promotes personal bonding with your tenants. It also saves an applicant from going through three screening processes – the agency's, yours, and that of the tenants who may already be residing at the rental property.

The most important thing you must do is to make good tenant selections. Direct that procedure yourself, as much as possible.

Organizational Housing Offices

Many organizations and institutions have housing referral offices – or, in the case of universities, off-campus housing offices. It usually takes just one phone call to list your house with that organization.

The housing office often has standard questions about your house and about the type of person you are looking for. There is no charge for this service. This use of housing offices is particularly effective if your rental house is near a:

- military base
- university
- large organization

Another advantage to using organizational housing offices is that you can target your potential renting audience. For example, you are most likely to wind up with a doctor or a medical student if you advertise at the medical school of a university; you are most likely to get military personnel if you advertise through the housing office of a military base.

There are few, if any, disadvantages to employing this method – it can be a really useful way to find tenants. It's free, quick, and easy. And, perhaps best of all – the applicants who respond will, to some extent, have been pre-selected by the kind of organizations with which you have chosen to list your property.

Notices on Bulletin Boards

Posting notices on bulletin boards is another free way to find tenants. You may want to post notices in some or all of the following places, if they are in close proximity to your house:

- libraries
- your place of work
- government office buildings
- churches, synagogues, and mosques
- clubs and associations
- book stores
- grocery stores
- ethnic or vegetarian restaurants
- health food stores
- apartment complexes – particularly those being converted to condominiums

Again, you can target your audience by posting your notice in places designed to attract a certain kind of person.

The chief drawback to this method is that it is time-consuming to compose the notices and run all over town posting them. Furthermore, you may want to check your notices every week or two to make sure they still have current information and that they haven't been taken down.

Signs

A very inexpensive way to advertise is to keep a display sign in the front of your property. You could keep the sign in the front window or have one mounted on the lawn. The quality of the sign displays the quality of the manager to many people, so make sure it looks professional.

The sign should be as simple as possible while still conveying your intended message. Use the sign in combination with other media (especially classified ads), since the number of people you can reach with a sign is obviously limited.

One advantage of using a sign is that, once made, it can be used over and over again at no additional cost to the owner.

Real Estate Brokers

Since real estate brokers are in constant contact with people in search of housing, their ability to find qualified tenants is quite good. Some realtors will also do credit checks on potential tenants before handing them over to you.

The problem with using real estate brokers is that they are expensive. You can often do the work yourself for much less than it would cost you to use a broker. A typical broker's finder's fee is 50% to 100% of one month's rent or 6% of the total lease.

Some charge even more than this, and for that reason you might want to consider using them only if the tenant is responsible for paying them.

Newspaper and Online Classifieds

You will probably get your quickest results by running a weekend ad in the classified section of the largest newspaper in your locality.

Look at the headings of the newspaper's classified section to determine where you should place your ad. Some of the usual categories are:

- "roommates"
- "rooms, houses, apartments to share"
- "apartments"
- "furnished apartments"

Newspapers may vary with the specific nomenclature they use to describe the categories.

You may want to take out a couple of ads. For example, you could place one under "Roommates" for the part of your rental house in which all facilities would be shared, and another under "Unfurnished Apartment" for the part of the house which has a private suite.

Or, for starters, you may decide to take out only one ad. You don't need a separate ad for each room you intend to rent. Advertise the least expensive area of the house, then show prospective tenants the other rooms of the house when they come.

Applicants often decide to take a more spacious room and pay a little more rent once they've seen the house.

Find out if the newspaper has special rates. Some newspapers substantially reduce their rates if you place a 3-line ad for 3 days, or a 2-line ad for a week. Generally, though, the weekend is the best time to run an ad.

If you have to choose one day, advertise in the Sunday edition. That way your advertisement will reach the most people.

The chief disadvantage of this method is that it costs money. If you have to run ads for a couple of months, the costs can add up quickly. The other disadvantage is that no matter how carefully you word your ad, you will usually get a very diverse collection of callers – which perhaps may include one or two obscene phone calls.

Nevertheless, the advantages of advertising in the newspaper outweigh the disadvantages. An ad in the classified section reaches far more people than does any other method. You just need the patience to screen the callers. Even if you have to spend a fair amount to advertise, it's worth the money to find good tenants as quickly as possible.

If you skimp on advertising and miss a month or more of rent, your loss of rental income will be far greater than your advertising expense would have been.

Similar to newspapers classified ads, many more renters are turning to the world wide web to find places to rent. It's free for them and they can access listings right away.

There are many free online classified sites with sections allowing landlords to post up vacancies and descriptions of properties, including photos of the property. Other sites that landlords can place ads are specific to rental properties. Some of these sites do not charge for listing a vacancy; however, others will charge a minimal fee. Viewers of online ads can contact the landlord via email or if the landlord opts to post their phone number, the potential tenant can contact the landlord directly.

Online classifieds benefit both the landlord and tenant because of the speed in which either party can post and access the information. The ad is often placed on the site right away, so there is no time in waiting for papers to be printed, and tenants can see the most recently posted ads.

HOW TO DESIGN AN ADVERTISEMENT

Advertisements should be designed to serve two purposes. The first purpose, of course, is to bring in phone calls from people you may want to have as tenants. The second purpose, however, is to screen out calls from people you think would not make good tenants.

It is therefore crucial for an advertisement to be as specific as possible without being wordy. A well-written ad will save you a lot of time from dealing with people who would not make suitable tenants. There is no need to write a long, extremely detailed advertisement, just provide the essential information. You can supply all of the details when people phone.

Here is what to include:

Location

After having checked under the proper heading, for example, "Furnished Apartments," the prospective tenant's next consideration is location. It should therefore be the first thing the ad mentions. It's usually enough to just give the general idea or major intersection, since the prospects will phone for directions (if they need them) before coming over.

Adjectives

It is best when describing the vacancy to use colourful words such as:

- spacious
- spotless
- quiet
- modern

These adjectives should honestly reflect the features of the vacancy. If they are misleading, the prospect will more than likely be disappointed upon personal inspection. The adjectives should stir up a positive mental picture of the property in the reader's mind.

Number of Rooms

It is sufficient to simply state the number of bedrooms, although some people prefer to give the total number of rooms. The bathroom should be excluded (unless there is more than one), but any special rooms that make the apartment or house sound more attractive (e.g. den, games room, sunroom, etc.) should definitely be noted.

Rent

Always include a rental rate in the ad. If you don't, you will be plagued with calls from people inquiring what the rate is. Many of these people may be expecting a bargain rate and are not really interested in the property.

Advertise your rents on a per week or a per month basis, depending on whether you want your tenants for the short or the long term. For leases of one year or more you should quote your rents on a per month basis. Since most apartments are rented on a monthly basis you can list the price without using the words "per month" in the ad.

It is important to write in the words "per week" if that is your intention, as the amount quoted could be mistaken for a bargain monthly rent.

Telephone Number

The telephone number of the person screening the tenants must be in the ad, because people will generally call before inspecting the property in person. This way you can explain more about the property than you could have possibly put in the ad and this will also allow the prospective tenants an opportunity to set up an appointment to view the apartment.

We will cover more about telephone calls from prospective tenants and setting up an answering machine to monitor those calls later in the chapter.

Open House

One alternative to putting your telephone number in the ad and dealing with these problems is to hold an open house. Advertise that the property will be open for viewing between specific hours on a certain night or weekend afternoon.

This way you can show the property to more than one person at a time. People will feel that they have to act fast if they are viewing the property with other prospective tenants. If you have an open house you should have an elaborate ad that details everything about your house, including good directions on how to get there. If you decide to include your telephone number, omit the directions and simply limit it to the specific details.

Specific Details

You may choose to include such extras as:

- pool
- garden
- play area
- fireplace
- appliances
- air conditioning
- type of tenant preferred

If you are going to allow pets, it is best to mention this in the advertisement, but if you are not going to allow them, you can leave this out altogether.

If utilities are going to be included in the price of rent, make sure to state this in the ad. You may decide to omit some of these specific details from the ad in order to save money when placing it – when the potential tenant phones you can then mention these details in order to encourage a visit.

Make sure that you do not repeat anything that the newspaper has already listed for you.

Here's an example: if your house is listed under the category "FURNISHED APARTMENTS FOR RENT" there is absolutely no need to include the words "furnished" or "apartment" in your ad.

Likewise, if the ads are grouped according to geographical location, for example, "WEST," then you do not need to mention in your ad that your rental property is in the western part of the city.

HELPFUL ABBREVIATIONS

The following is a list of abbreviations that you can use in your ads. It is important to note that you should not overuse them, as your ad could become indecipherable, especially to those not very familiar with rental ad lingo.

❏	cac	central air-conditioning
❏	wwc	wall-to-wall carpets
❏	w/d	washer/dryer
❏	apt	apartment
❏	bsmt	basement
❏	br	bedroom
❏	ba	bathroom
❏	fpl	fireplace
❏	yd	yard
❏	shr	share
❏	w	with
❏	nr	near

THE TELEPHONE AND THE ANSWERING MACHINE

If you are the manager of several rental properties or units, you may want to install a separate telephone line in your house to be used only for business purposes. This way you won't bother the rest of your household with what might be an abundance of business calls. This phone line would also be tax-deductible as a business expense.

You should install the business line in a quiet, secluded area of the house – perhaps in a study or in a finished basement. Place the phone on a desk, within easy reach of the files you maintain for your properties.

It is also strongly recommended that you buy an answering machine. If you don't, you'll have to spend weekends and evenings in the proximity of your telephone while awaiting the calls. You may also have meals interrupted by telephone calls.

With an answering machine, you can:

- schedule a time to return calls at your convenience
- record essential information, including the caller's name, home phone number, and office phone number
- reduce the number of obscene calls you receive

A useful feature for any answering machine is that which allows you to phone your answering machine from another telephone to check your messages. If you're working another job, this would allow you to check your calls during lunch break.

In addition, if away from home you can still keep up-to-date on possible cancellations from potential tenants regarding showings of the rental property.

Another option is to use a mobile phone to manage your business, which is fairly common today. This provides you the convenience of having your phone with you at all times, thereby not missing any important calls and being able to pick up messages promptly. However, there are a few inconveniences of using your mobile phone for business (particularly if you also use it for personal calls). First, you may not know if someone is calling regarding a property or an ad you placed or if it is a personal call coming in. This means you will have to answer your phone professionally at all times. Second, if you do not have an answering machine, you will miss calls. Third, if you do have an answering machine, you will have to have a professional message as your recording which you may not like as your standard recording, since you may also be using the mobile phone as your personal phone.

Your Message

Keep your message short and friendly, and try to avoid being cute or apologetic about using an answering machine.

Here's an example of a good message, assuming your name is Gord:

"Hello, and thanks for calling. You've reached Gord's answering machine. If you're calling about the ad for the apartment, it is still available. I can't come to the phone right now, but I would like to speak to you. At the sound of the tone, please leave your name and number both at home and at work, and I'll get back to you as soon as possible. Thank you very much."

The Obscene Phone Caller

You should be prepared for the possibility of receiving a couple of obscene phone calls, even if you have an answering machine.

Receiving obscene phone calls can be unnerving at first, but after a while you will most likely become bored with them.

Here's a good way to handle the call: as soon as you realize the nature of the call, don't say a word. Simply put the phone down off the receiver and walk away. When it finally sinks in that nobody is listening, the caller will most likely hang up.

Don't act scared or hang up in a panic, and don't talk to the person. If you react to the caller in any way, he may continue to harass you. Do not blow a whistle in their ear. If you do, the caller may phone you back at 3 o'clock in the morning and blow a whistle back at you. If it is an obscene call from a tenant, record it for future needs.

Keep a List of Callers

By all means, keep track of the people who phone. List them in a single notebook, not on scraps of paper or in the margins of your personal day planner. Your notebook could have pages with the following columns:

- date
- person's name
- home telephone number
- office telephone number
- comments
- appointment

You will get information for the first four columns from the recorded message left on your answering machine. You'll be able to fill in the comments column when you speak with the caller and find out more information about the person. Jot down in the appointment column the time that they show up.

The list of callers can be useful to you in other ways, too. You will know how to get in touch with a prospective tenant for follow-up if the caller misses an appointment or if you need to change or confirm an appointment.

You'll also have a list ready when the time comes to inform all the applicants as to whether they have been accepted as tenants. Furthermore, if a tenant in one of your houses unexpectedly moves out within a month or so, you may check the list for a person you liked but did not choose as a tenant. Even if that person has already taken other accommodations, he may know of others who are looking for places to rent.

WHAT TO SAY TO POTENTIAL TENANTS ON THE PHONE

You should be able to do a lot of your screening on the telephone. The more thorough your screening is over the telephone, the more time you will save by only showing the house to reasonably good prospects.

You do not necessarily want a lot of people to come to look at your rental property; you want only a few, well-screened prospects who have a pretty good possibility of becoming tenants.

What should you say to your callers that will sound friendly, yet will effectively screen them, while not sounding like you are prying? Perhaps try to put yourself in their shoes. It may help to address their concerns first, before asking them questions about themselves.

When potential tenants phone, they will want to know more about the house; they will want to know if they will feel comfortable with any others who may be living in the household; and they will want to know more about the rental terms.

At this point it will help to have prepared a list of all the relevant information about the rental property. This way you can immediately ask the callers whether they have specific questions or would prefer to hear a running monologue of all the relevant information. Most will opt for the monologue.

Let the callers know everything about the property: positive, negative, or neutral. Explain the characteristics of tenants you'd like to have in the household. This could be something such as relatively quiet people who like to be in a house that's clean, reasonably tidy, and who are considerate of others.

Then you should describe the most and least attractive features of the house. Existing attractive features, for example, could be the white brick fireplace, the beamed ceiling in the living room, the washer and dryer, and the fact that public transportation and shopping are within a short walking distance.

Unattractive features may consist of such things as a relatively small bedroom, small closets, and the fact that the property is on a busy street.

If you are honest about the drawbacks, you will achieve three positive results:

1) The prospective tenants will identify you as a trustworthy person.
2) When the prospective tenants come to look at the house, they

will be prepared for the worst, and so they will often wind up reassuring you that the problem isn't really that bad.
3) If a caller absolutely needs a large bedroom because he or she has a king-size bed, two bureaus, and a gigantic desk, there is no sense in wasting your time and his by setting up an appointment. Therefore you save your time and theirs.

Finish up your running monologue by describing the most crucial terms of the rental agreement, whatever you desire them to be. Such terms could include:

- the duration of the tenant's stay
- paying first and last month's rent
- a security deposit
- your rental system
- additional costs for utilities

In the final part of your monologue, you may want to add that the vacancy will not necessarily be filled on a first-come, first-served basis and that you will be taking the time to meet with many (if not all) prospective tenants before arriving at a final decision.

There are a variety of reasons for mentioning this:

- Callers should not feel as though they have to make an appointment with you immediately – this may only result in over-booking your schedule
- You will be able to meet with all of the prospective tenants, increasing your chances of finding the ideal ones
- You may desire some breathing space before making a final decision

Although you have put together your remarks as a monologue, the caller will most likely interrupt you several times with questions and comments. This is good—you are establishing a rapport.

If you are requesting a security deposit, this may dissuade some potential tenants right away. Others may have problems with rules you insist upon, or the general location. Callers who would not make suitable tenants often screen themselves out. This self-screening is to your mutual benefit.

You can even pause at some point to inquire as to whether anything you've said has dulled their interest. If they respond with a "no," then ask if they have any questions about anything you haven't mentioned. If so, answer those questions to the best of your ability.

With all of their concerns out of the way, it's your turn to do some inquiring. You could say, "Now, do you mind if I ask you some questions about yourself?"

SCREENING CRITERIA

These are all aspects of the potential tenant that you should know:

- age
- type of work
- hours of work
- length of time employed
- length of time in area
- length of time in current residence
- reason for wanting to leave current residence
- smoker or non-smoker
- ownership or non-ownership of pets
- ability to pay the rent and the initial deposit (or first/last month)
- expected length of residence as your tenant

The three most significant aspects you should be on the lookout for are:

1) Has this individual been steadily employed and, if so, for how long?
2) Why is he leaving his current residence, how long did he live there, and how did he get along there?
3) Is this individual willing and able to pay first/last month and/or the security deposit?

Depending on the situation, you may choose to be somewhat flexible with one of these elements. You might take on an unemployed tenant with a big bank account, or you might figure out a system wherein a tenant pays the initial deposit over a two-month period.

You might deduce that a potential tenant has a justifiable reason for not getting along well in his or her last residence. Perhaps the individual's roommates were wild party-lovers who would stay up all night listening to outrageous music. On the other hand, he/she might have been living in a bad and intimidating area.

However, if you totally overlook any of those three aspects, you may be in for some unpleasant surprises after the tenant moves in.

Basically, what you're searching for amongst the potential tenants is stability – personal stability in their places of residence and their places of employment.

BE AWARE OF THESE POTENTIAL TENANTS

The Potential Tenant who Wants to Move in Immediately

Look out for the caller who wants to move into your rental property right away. The only exception you might want to make would be for somebody who has just come into town and is staying at a hotel or motel.

In most situations, tenants have to give at least 60 days notice before leaving their current residence. If they are prepared to move at a moment's notice, this could mean that they are:

- being evicted
- having serious problems with one or more people in their current residence
- impulsive by nature, perhaps likely to move out of your house on the spur of the moment, too

The Potential Tenant who Wants to See the Property Immediately

Although most, if not all of your callers, may ask for the specific location of your rental property, you shouldn't give them an address until you have completed your screening and you are sure you want to show them the property.

Beware of callers who want to know the address and come over immediately without even having asked you any questions about the property. There is an air of desperation in such a request, and a desperate tenant is not really what you want – he may say whatever you want to hear, and not be totally honest. They may also accept terms or rules which they will have trouble dealing with in reality.

The potential tenants you are most likely to want will ask you thorough questions about the property and the rental terms before deciding whether or not they want to see the property.

The Potential Tenant who Moves or Changes Jobs Frequently

Be wary of the potential tenant who has had more than two jobs or more than two places of residence in the past year.

Often, such a person has some personal or economic problem that is at the root of this instability. Still, don't be afraid to use your own judgment in this sort of situation: if the reasons the individual gives for the changes seem realistic and understandable, you may want to at least show the property to the caller.

The Potential Tenant who Disputes the Deposit Requirement

If after you've explained the reasons why you need the first and last months' rents up front, along with the security deposit (if applicable), and the potential tenant responds that he personally doesn't see any reason for these safety precautions because he is a trustworthy person, this may indicate that the individual is, in fact, not a trustworthy person.

If someone argues with you over this point, it may be most prudent to simply explain that although what you're asking for is a significant amount of money, it's a requirement for all of your tenants. Thank the person for calling, tell them you're sorry it's not going to work out, and say goodbye. Either the person will have to look elsewhere for a place to stay, or he may turn suddenly on their heels and agree to the deposit requirement. You should still remain wary of this person if you do decide to show him the property.

The individual who argues about the deposit will likely be the first person to damage the house and move out without notice. Good tenants will understand the risks of renting out property to others and will therefore understand why you need the deposit.

Good tenants will have enough commitment to stay with you and be a good tenant, so they won't object to the deposit.

The Potential Tenant Currently Living with Friends or Family

When potential tenants let it be known that they are currently living with friends or family, find out for how long they have been in that situation, and exactly why.

Sometimes, people who have just been evicted or have just come out of a mental health or correctional facility have no other place to go but to family and friends. Their backgrounds may or may not exclude them from being your tenant, but you should be aware of them and any potential problems.

However, students or young people making their initial move away from home may be an exception you will want to consider.

The Potential Tenant who is Between Jobs

For obvious financial reasons, it makes the most sense to search for a full-time worker or a full-time student, someone who will be able to afford to live at your rental property. As previously mentioned, there could be exceptions. For example, an affluent individual with a lot of money in the bank might be an exception you would consider.

The Potential Tenant Who Objects to Personal Questions

It is important for a tenant and landlord to have open and honest communication from the very beginning. It is crucial to get a housing and employment history, and sometimes to get more personal information if, from the conversation, you sense something such as the individual considering having his/her girlfriend/boyfriend move in at some point.

The person who is offended by your questions (assuming they are relevant and in good taste) will probably not make a good tenant.

The Potential Tenant who Owns a "Junky" Car

Look out for potential tenants who arrive in "junky" cars. This doesn't mean old cars. It means cars with:

- smashed headlights
- badly dented doors
- torn seats
- accumulated trash scattered on the floor

It is logical to believe that a tenant with a "junky" car will look after your rental property in a similar manner.

SCHEDULING AN APPOINTMENT TO SEE THE RENTAL PROPERTY

After having screened a potential tenant over the phone and determining the caller might be suitable to rent to, make an appointment for that person to see the house and to meet you.

Schedule several appointments together and give each person a specified time. Make sure you are giving yourself enough time to show the property to each individual. By scheduling the appointments together, you will use your time most wisely.

Some landlords may promote scheduling several potential tenants at the same time in order to make the applicants feel the pressure of competition, but this may not be the in your best interest. You wouldn't be able to spend any time apart getting to know the prospective tenants as individuals, which might have very well affected your decision.

Hopefully, you will have a business relationship with that individual for some time. You want your tenants to feel comfortable with you, and a first impression can be lasting.

HOW TO CUT DOWN ON NO-SHOWS

Inevitably, some of the people you have scheduled to look at the rental property won't show up for the appointment. This can be frustrating, because you may end up wasting half-an-hour waiting for nothing, when you could have scheduled someone else to see the place during that period.

You can reduce the number of no-shows by carefully asking the applicant to phone you and let you know if anything comes up that is going to keep them from making the appointment. The same goes with showing up late. Once someone has verbally promised to let you know if they aren't coming, they are much more likely to do so if the situation arises.

SHOWING THE PROPERTY TO POTENTIAL TENANTS

Make a list of all of the potential tenants whom you have scheduled, and greet everyone at the door as they show up for their appointments. Show the callers the entire house, and make sure to point out all the convenient features and amenities.

If you have made plans to upgrade the house or to make specific repairs, let the potential tenants know what you plan on doing and when you intend to do it.

SAYING YES TO A POTENTIAL TENANT

It might be prudent to hold off on trying to make a decision right there and then – the same goes for having the tenant make a decision on the spot. Both of you should have time to contemplate and think the decision over.

And if you've told prospective tenants that you are not operating on a first-come, first-served basis, then it is only fair to stick by your word and meet all of the prospective tenants.

If you do think that an individual would make an excellent tenant, you may want to say something such as, "I like you, and think that you would work out well as a tenant. I don't know if this place is something you might be interested in."

If the individual responds by saying that he/she is quite interested in the place, ask him/her if you can phone them back the next evening at a predetermined time with a final decision.

SAYING NO TO A POTENTIAL TENANT

Fortunately, human nature is often such that if you are not getting along especially well with a potential tenant, he will feel somewhat the same way. Such an individual may let you know that he still has other places to see.

How do you turn down an individual who wants to rent from you? First of all, explain that you have promised to show the house to others, and that no decision will be made until you have seen everyone. Let him know when you will phone with a decision. Then make sure to phone at the promised time.

When you call, make sure to explain to the individual that you appreciated having him come and look at the house, but that someone else was selected. If you have more than one vacancy at a rental property (and the prospective tenant knows this), this explanation may not suffice.

Try to think of an honest reason why you think things wouldn't work out – hopefully without hurting the individual. Here are some examples:

- Given the nature of the person's job, you weren't sure that he/she would stay for very long.
- His work hours might bother other tenants in the house, if it is to be shared.
- You weren't in favour of having a baby grand piano moved into the living room of your rental property.

If you can't think of anything else, just say that you're sorry, and you're not sure you can explain why, but you feel somehow things wouldn't work out.

Or, say that because you would like to interview more applicants, you plan to run the ad for a few more weekends. As a kindness to the person, though, you may want to let him know as nicely as you can that he is out of the running. Honesty that is not tinged with emotion, and is not judgmental, is usually appreciated.

RENTAL APPLICATIONS

Before you decide that you would like to make a prospective tenant into a current tenant, you will want that individual to fill out a rental application, which will provide:

- personal information
- employment information
- credit information

Then to make sure that the information is truthful, you will want to follow up on the employment information and credit information.

An example of a rental application, along with an employment verification inquiry letter and a credit check inquiry letter are provided in the following pages.

You can use these as templates in the future for your own applications and letters.

RENTAL APPLICATION

Prospective Address: _____

Desired Date of Occupancy: _____

Desired Length of Occupancy: _____

Prospective Tenant: _____

S.I.N. # _____ DL# _____

DOB (D/M/Y): ____/____/____

Mother's Maiden Name: _____

Home Phone: _____ Alternate Phone: _____

Current Address: _____

City: _____ Province: _____ Postal Code: _____

How long have you been residing at this address? _____

Reason for moving: _____

Name of Landlord (if applicable): _____

Landlord's Phone (if applicable): _____

Previous Address: _____

City: _____ Province: _____ Postal Code: _____

How long have you been residing at this address? _____

Reason for moving: _____

Name of Landlord (if applicable): _____

Landlord's Phone (if applicable): _____

Make, Model & Year of Car: _____

License Plate # _____

Sample Rental Application Form

EMPLOYMENT

Current Employer: _____

Supervisor Name: _____

Position: _____

Phone Number: _____

Employed from _____ to _____

Reason for leaving (if applicable) _____

Previous Employer: _____

Supervisor Name: _____

Position: _____

Phone Number: _____

Employed from _____ to _____

Reason for leaving _____

MONTHLY INCOME

Source: [ ] wages   [ ] salary   [ ] commission   [ ] tips

[ ] government assistance   [ ] other _____

Monthly Take-Home Pay (Net, after taxes): _____

Sample Rental Application Form

Prospective Co-Tenant: _____

S.I.N. # _____ DL# _____

DOB (D/M/Y): _____/_____/_____

Mother's Maiden Name: _____

Home Phone: _____ Alternate Phone: _____

Current Address: _____

City: _____ Province: _____ Postal Code: _____

How long have you been residing at this address? _____

Reason for moving: _____

Name of Landlord (if applicable): _____

Landlord's Phone (if applicable): _____

Previous Address: _____

City: _____ Province: _____ Postal Code: _____

How long have you been residing at this address? _____

Reason for moving: _____

Name of Landlord (if applicable): _____

Landlord's Phone (if applicable): _____

Make, Model & Year of Car: _____

License Plate # _____

Sample Rental Application Form

EMPLOYMENT

Current Employer: _____

Supervisor Name: _____

Position: _____

Phone Number: _____

Employed from _____ to _____

Reason for leaving (if applicable) _____

Previous Employer: _____

Supervisor Name: _____

Position: _____

Phone Number: _____

Employed from _____ to _____

Reason for leaving _____

MONTHLY INCOME

Source: [ ] wages   [ ] salary   [ ] commission   [ ] tips

[ ] government assistance   [ ] other _____

Monthly Take-Home Pay (Net, after taxes): _____

Sample Rental Application Form

Other Tenants	Age	Relationship	Occupation

LEARNED SKILLS

[ ] Plumbing [ ] Electrical [ ] Painting [ ] Carpentry

[ ] Roofing [ ] Cement Work [ ] Appliance Repair

[ ] Other _____

PETS

Pet Name	Type/Breed	Size	Gender	Indoor/Outdoor

CREDIT REFERENCES, BANKS, & CREDIT

Creditor	Address/ Phone	Limit	Purpose	Account Open?

Bank	Type of Account	Balance	Account Number	Account Holders

Credit Card	Limit	Balance	Account Number	Account Holders

Sample Rental Application Form

PERSONAL REFERENCES

Name	Address	City	Phone	Relationship

NEXT OF KIN/EMERGENCY CONTACT

Name	Address	City	Phone	Relationship

Do you own any real estate?　　　　　　　　　　　[ ] yes　[ ] no
　　If yes, what kind of real estate and where is it located?
　　_____

Have you ever been evicted from any tenancy?　　　[ ] yes　[ ] no

Have you ever wilfully/intentionally refused to pay rent when due?
　　　　　　　　　　　　　　　　　　　　　　　　[ ] yes　[ ] no

Do you know of anything that may interrupt your income or ability to pay rent?　　　　　　　　　　　　　　　　　　　　[ ] yes　[ ] no

---

I hereby certify that the answers I have given in this application are true and correct to the best of my knowledge. I understand that any false answers or statements made by me will be sufficient grounds for eviction and loss of any security deposit.

[Optional:]

Applicant permits and agrees to pay a fee of $ _____ for a credit check to be performed on himself/herself and the co-occupant by their signatures below:

Date: _____

Prospective Tenant: _____

Prospective Co-Tenant: _____

Sample Rental Application Form

(Date)

(Employer's name)
(Employer's address)
(Employer's city, province, postal code)

REFERENCE: (Name of Prospective Tenant)

Dear Sir/Madame:

(Name of prospective tenant) has given me your name as his employer on an application to rent a dwelling located at (address of your property, city, province, postal code).

He/she claims that his/her job position is (give his job title), and his salary is $ (figure given to you) per (week or month), and that he has worked for you from (starting date) to the present.

Please supply the following information by phone or complete the questions on the following page attached to this letter and return it to me. My phone number is (phone #). The best time to reach me is (give times).

Thank you very much for your co-operation.

Sincerely yours,

(your name)

Sample Employment Verification Inquiry Letter

EMPLOYMENT VERIFICATION QUESTIONS
(Sent as separate page along with letter or as separate attachment with an email.)

1. Is he/she currently your employee?   Yes   No

2. What is his/her job title? _____

3. What is his/her salary or hourly wage? $ _____ salary hourly

4. How long has he/she worked for you? _____

_____   _____
Name   Title

_____
Date

Sample Employment Verification Inquiry Letter

(Date)

(Creditor's name)
(Creditor's address)
(Creditor's city, province, postal code)

REFERENCE: (Name of prospective tenant)

Dear Sir/Madame:

(Name of prospective tenant) has given me your name as a credit reference on an application to rent a dwelling located at (address of your property, city, province, postal code).

He/she claims that they have a loan or bill outstanding with you in the amount of $ (figure given you) and that his payments are $ (figure given you) per month.

Please supply the following information by phone or complete the questions on the following page attached to this letter and return it to me. My phone number is (phone #). The best time to reach me is (give times).

Thank you very much for your co-operation.

Sincerely yours,

(your name)

Sample Credit Check Inquiry Letter

CREDIT CHECK INQUIRY QUESTIONS
(Sent as separate page along with letter or as separate attachment with an email.)

1. How much does he/she owe you?
   _____

2. What are his/her payments per month?
   _____

3. Is he/she late or delinquent in payments?
   _____

4. Describe his/her payment history?
   _____
   _____

_____   _____
Name   Title

_____
Date

Sample Credit Check Inquiry Letter

LANDLORD/TENANT UNIT INSPECTION

The following form can be used by both the landlord and the tenant moving into a property. It is a good idea to use this or something similar when doing a walk through of a property so that when you walk away, you have a document/checklist to reference and both parties signing to it agree on the condition of the property.

LANDLORD/TENANT UNIT INSPECTION INVENTORY

Unit Address: _____

GRADING SYSTEM
A = excellent   B = good   C = mediocre   D = somewhat deficient
F = totally unsatisfactory   N / A = not applicable

COMMON AREAS			
Area/Item	**Grade**	**Landlord Initials**	**Tenant Initials**
Front hallway			
Floor and/or carpet			
Walls			
Ceiling			
Stairwells			
Lights			
Front door			
Rear door			
Thermostat			

LIVING ROOM			
Area/Item	**Grade**	**Landlord Initials**	**Tenant Initials**
Windows			
Walls			
Ceiling			
Doors			
Floor and/or Carpet			
Bookcase			
Fireplace			
Lights			
Other:			
Other:			

KITCHEN			
Area/Item	**Grade**	**Landlord Initials**	**Tenant Initials**
Counters			
Sinks			
Cupboards			
Drawers			
Windows			
Floor			
Walls			
Ceiling			
Doors			
Table			
Stove			
Refrigerator			
Microwave			
Lights			
Other:			
Other:			

Sample Landlord/Tenant Unit Inspection Inventory

DINING ROOM

Area/Item	Grade	Landlord Initials	Tenant Initials
Floor and/or carpet			
Windows			
Walls			
Ceiling			
Doors			
Hanging light			
Other:			
Other:			

MASTER BEDROOM

Area/Item	Grade	Landlord Initials	Tenant Initials
Floor and/or carpet			
Windows			
Walls			
Ceiling			
Doors			
Light			
Closet			
Drapes/Curtains			
Other:			
Other:			

SECOND BEDROOM

Area/Item	Grade	Landlord Initials	Tenant Initials
Floor and/or carpet			
Windows			
Walls			
Ceiling			
Doors			
Light			
Closet			
Drapes/Curtains			
Other:			
Other:			

THIRD BEDROOM

Area/Item	Grade	Landlord Initials	Tenant Initials
Floor and/or carpet			
Windows			
Walls			
Ceiling			
Doors			
Light			
Closet			
Drapes/Curtains			
Other:			
Other:			

Sample Landlord/Tenant Unit Inspection Inventory

FIRST BATHROOM			
Area/Item	Grade	Landlord Initials	Tenant Initials
Floor			
Windows			
Walls			
Ceiling			
Doors			
Light			
Sink			
Toilet Tank			
Toilet Seat			
Toilet Bowl			
Shower (door/curtain)			
Shower Walls			
Shower Head/Hose/Faucet			
Bathtub			
Towel Rack(s)			
Counter			
Cabinet			
Mirror			
Other:			
Other:			

SECOND BATHROOM			
Area/Item	Grade	Landlord Initials	Tenant Initials
Floor			
Windows			
Walls			
Ceiling			
Doors			
Light			
Sink			
Toilet Tank			
Toilet Seat			
Toilet Bowl			
Shower (door/curtain)			
Shower Walls			
Shower Head/Hose/Faucet			
Bathtub			
Towel Rack(s)			
Counter			
Cabinet			
Mirror			
Other:			
Other:			

Sample Landlord/Tenant Unit Inspection Inventory

PRACTICAL PROPERTY MANAGEMENT

BASEMENT/LAUNDRY			
Area/Item	**Grade**	**Landlord Initials**	**Tenant Initials**
Floor			
Windows			
Walls			
Ceiling			
Doors			
Light			
Furnace			
Washer			
Dryer			
Chest Freezer			
Mirror			
Other:			
Other:			

OTHER AREAS/ITEMS			
Area/Item	**Grade**	**Landlord Initials**	**Tenant Initials**
Other:			
Other:			
Other:			
Other:			
Other:			
Other:			

Smoke Detectors on all floors & working?　　　　Yes　　No
　　　　　　　　　　　　　　Type:　　　　Battery　Electric

Carbon Monoxide Detectors on all floors & working?　Yes　　No
　　　　　　　　　　　　　　Type:　　　　Battery　Electric

The rental unit conditions are confirmed as of the date noted by our signatures below.

Date: _____

Landlord: _____　　Tenant: _____

Sample Landlord/Tenant Unit Inspection Inventory

LANDLORD/TENANT INVENTORY FOR FURNISHED UNITS

Some landlords decide that they want to offer furnished units. This will depend on the target audience and area of the rental property. The following form can be used by both the landlord and the tenant moving into a furnished property. It serves as a document that both the landlord and tenant agree on for what is contained in the unit and notes on the condition of the property.

LANDLORD/TENANT INVENTORY
FOR FURNISHED UNITS

LIVING ROOM	
Item	Condition/Comment
Tables	
Chairs	
Mirrors	
Sofas	
Lamps	
Bookcases	
AV Equipment	
TV/VCR/DVD	
Stereo System	
Pictures/Paintings	
Curtains/Blinds	

KITCHEN	
Item	Condition/Comment
Tables	
Chairs	
Cutlery & Other Utensils	
Pots & Pans	
Toaster	
Microwave	
Blender	
Coffee Maker	
Other:	

DINING ROOM	
Item	Condition/Comment
Tables	
Chairs	
Table Covering	
Placemats	
Cloth Napkins	
Silverware	
Curtains/Drapes	
Dinnerware & Glassware	
Ornaments	
Candleholders	
Pictures/Paintings	
Lights	
Other:	

Sample Landlord/Tenant Inventory For Furnished Units

MASTER BEDROOM	
Item	Condition/Comment
Bed(s)	
Chairs	
Tables	
Dressers/Chests	
Bedding	
Mirrors	
Lamps	
Clock/Radio	
Other:	

SECOND BEDROOM	
Item	Condition/Comment
Bed(s)	
Chairs	
Tables	
Dressers/Chests	
Bedding	
Mirrors	
Lamps	
Clock/Radio	
Other:	

THIRD BEDROOM	
Item	Condition/Comment
Bed(s)	
Chairs	
Tables	
Dressers/Chests	
Bedding	
Mirrors	
Lamps	
Clock/Radio	
Other:	

FIRST BATHROOM	
Item	Condition/Comment
Towels	
Facecloths	
Shower Curtain/Liner	
Mats	
Scale	
Medicine Cabinet	
Lights	
Sink	
Tub	

Sample Landlord/Tenant Inventory For Furnished Units

SECOND BATHROOM	
Item	Condition/Comment
Towels	
Facecloths	
Shower Curtain/Liner	
Mats	
Scale	
Medicine Cabinet	
Lights	
Sink	
Tub	

BASEMENT, LAUNDRY ROOM & ATTIC	
Item	Condition/Comment
Tools	
Brooms/Mops	
Vacuum Cleaner	
Washer/Dryer	
Other Cleaning Equipment	
Washer	
Dryer	
Iron	
Other:	

GARAGE & OUTBUILDINGS	
Item	Condition/Comment
Workbench	
Lawnmower	
Snow Blower	
Hardware/Tools	
Garden Tools	
Lawn/Patio Furniture	
Other:	

The rental unit conditions are confirmed as of the date noted by our signatures below.

Date: _____

Landlord: _____   Tenant: _____

Sample Landlord/Tenant Inventory For Furnished Units

Chapter 3:

Leases

THE LEASE DOCUMENT

A lease is essentially an agreement between a landlord (lessor) and a tenant (lessee) for the use of a property for housing purposes. It can be written (this is recommended), oral, or implied.

Normally any lease lasting over a year is put down in writing. Shorter leases (monthly, weekly) are more likely to be verbal or implied.

The purpose of having a written lease as opposed to an oral one is that it clarifies the legal and other terms of the agreement. A properly worded lease will serve and guard the landlord against having a bad tenant living in his/her property.

It is best to keep the lease in straightforward and simple English, avoiding complicated legal terminology. If it's too complicated to understand, it may not stand up in court.

The lease document indicates the rights and duties of the parties involved and will act as a regulating guide throughout the relationship, thus giving a clear record of the intent of both parties.

It is important to note that the lease is a legal document: it is a written contract whereby one party gives to another the right to utilize a property for a certain duration of time.

The law relating to contracts of this nature has its very own terminology and varies somewhat from province to province and time to time as it is modified by legislation or interpretation. For these reasons it is useful to have legal advice before committing oneself to a specific form.

If there is a local apartment owners' association in your area, ask to see their standard leases. They may be exactly what you're looking for. There are different leases for different types of properties, all of which are fairly similar:

- house leases
- apartment leases

- commercial leases
- farm leases

THE CONSEQUENCES OF A WRITTEN DOCUMENT

The advantages of a written lease are two-fold:

1) A written document will reduce misunderstandings. It clearly sets forth the complete understanding, by each party involved, of the aspects relating to rights, privileges and obligations.
2) It also acts as a permanent record of the agreement.

A written lease is crucial for legal purposes. The Statute of Frauds requires most leases to be in writing if they are to be held enforceable by the courts. This statute, an antique English conception, can have an impact in two different ways:

1) It requires that contracts relating to the transference of land be in writing to be enforceable.
2) It requires that contracts that cannot be performed within a 12-month period be in writing in order to be enforceable.

The Statute of Frauds does not necessarily make a contract null and void or invalid, but rather states that, in the event of dispute and litigation, the courts of authority will not enforce an agreement falling under the statute unless it is in writing.

The initial purpose behind this was to avoid relying upon the memories of the parties or witnesses to the agreement who might, for example, have moved or died and become unavailable.

Its purpose is still to avoid future misunderstanding by requiring a written record of the agreement between the parties. The Statute of Frauds may vary as jurisdictions do, but, in general, the provisions are as indicated here.

TYPES OF LEASES

The sort of lease utilized depends on the type of property being managed. A prepared property manager should be knowledgeable in three basic types of leases:

- Gross Lease
- Net Lease
- Percentage Lease

In the following section we will look at each of these kinds of leases in detail.

GROSS LEASE

The most frequently used tenancy agreement is in the form of a gross lease; that is, the tenants pay a fixed rental and the owner covers all of the expenses which are associated with the operation of the property, including:

- Taxes
- Insurance
- Utilities
- Other expenses

In some cases, responsibility for utility costs and extraordinary repairs may be negotiated between the parties.

NET LEASE

The second type of lease is the net lease, under which the tenant not only pays the rent, but in addition to this, also assumes responsibility for certain expenses associated with the leased premises.

The landlord then receives a net figure as rent. Within this type there are three sub-types of net leases:

- Single-net lease
- Net-net lease

- Net-net-net lease (triple net lease)

SINGLE-NET LEASE

Under the single-net lease the tenant pays for the maintenance and operating expenses associated with the space being leased.

NET-NET LEASE

Under the net-net lease the tenant pays all the maintenance and operating expenses, plus the property taxes.

NET-NET-NET LEASE

Under the net-net-net lease (also known as the triple-net lease) the tenant pays all maintenance and operating expenses, property taxes and the insurance.

The net lease and its variations are usually long-term leases that have been designed for commercial properties such as large office buildings. Landlords and tenants are cautioned, however, to be extremely careful with these general interpretations in order to avoid any false assumptions.

Property managers should make sure to establish a very clear understanding between all parties concerned before relying on any sub-definitions. Some good advice: use only the phrase "net lease" and make sure to define it. It means that the tenant is responsible for paying all operating expenses, property taxes, and insurance.

PERCENTAGE LEASE

The third type of lease is the percentage lease, which is utilized for retail properties. The rental in a percentage lease is usually based on a percentage of gross sales or net income earned on the premises or a minimum fixed rent, whichever is greater.

With this type of lease, the landlord shares in the financial benefits of the leased premises. In contrast with the percentage lease, major retail tenants often negotiate a lease with a fixed charge per square foot.

There are also different combinations of the aforementioned leases, the most common being the gross lease. It has escalator clauses for certain expenses. Such a lease will establish the ceiling of the landlord's contribution – either by reference to a specific amount of money or time frame, with the tenant being obliged to pay any excess amount.

Residential properties in Canada most often use the gross lease concept, but it may come with an assortment of small variations.

Commercial buildings and office buildings commonly utilize a gross lease with an escalation provision for taxes and maintenance over a fixed base year. This includes direct payment for electrical consumption on either a measured or estimated basis.

Recently, there has been a growing trend towards complete triple-net leases. They have also been used effectively and profitably in retail properties, including shopping centres. Triple-net leases usually come in combination with a percentage clause.

THE ELEMENTS OF A VALID LEASE

There are six fundamental elements in a valid lease:

1) A statement of the correct name and signatures of the legally competent parties.
2) The inclusion of an easily recognizable description of the leased premises and its condition.
3) A statement of the consideration that supports the agreement, i.e., the rental payment and conveyance or demising clauses.
4) Legality of use; a statement of the purpose for which the premises are to be used and who may use them.
5) A statement of the commencement and expiration dates.
6) A statement of the rights and obligations of the parties.

THE CONTRACTING PARTIES

The first necessary element of a valid lease is a statement of the correct names and signatures of the legally competent contracting parties. The competency of a party is controlled by the law of the local authority and may vary from province to province.

Questions of competency arise from the law relating to contracts, as well as, agency (legal representation).

Minors

In all jurisdictions, minors (those beneath the age of legal competency) are considered incompetent to enter into a contractual bond. The definition of a minor may vary among jurisdictions, but in most cases the age of competency is 18 years.

Contracts entered into by minors are considered voidable, but not void or invalid. This means an adult contracting with a minor is obliged by all the terms and conditions of the agreement for as long as the minor chooses to seek execution of the agreement.

The minor, on the other hand, may renounce and void the agreement at any time while still a minor. In most jurisdictions, if a contracting party does not void an agreement entered into with a minor, within a reasonable period of time after the minor reaches the age of majority, this will act as reaffirmation of the agreement by a new capable party, thereby creating a valid and enforceable contract for both parties.

Insanity or Senility

In all jurisdictions an insane or senile party is held legally incompetent with the same protections afforded the minor. This consideration can become important when dealing with the elderly, with patients in a nursing home, and so forth.

If a question relating to capability seems likely to arise as a possible consideration, it is wise to have a physician witness the execution of the agreement. It is also a good idea to secure an affidavit concerning the competency of the party by that physician.

Corporations

In all jurisdictions, corporations are regarded as persons (an individual entity) in their own right competent to enter into a contractual relationship. However, the corporation can act only through its agents: generally, its directors and officers.

These corporate agents are considered competent to act only if they have received proper authority to enter into the contractual relationship. This authority may be granted either specifically by the corporate charter, or, as is more often the case, by declaration of the directors acting under general charter power.

Persons dealing with a corporation should be alerted to the fact that they are dealing with agents. Therefore, when involved in a lease with a corporate entity, it is always wise to ask that a certified copy of the resolution of the directors sanctioning the lease be attached to the document.

The Statute of Frauds requires that the lease agreement be in writing to be enforceable. The authority conferred upon the corporate agent seeking to execute the lease must also be in writing.

In order to bind a corporation to a lease, several things must occur:

- confirmation of the resolution of the directors
- signature by the duly chosen and authorized officer of the corporation on the lease
- confirmation by the secretary, to the duly appointed and authorized officer's signature
- affixing of the corporate seal

Agents Signing on Behalf of their Principals

In order for an agent to bind the principal, authority must have been received from the principal. Comments made with regard to corporate agents are equally applicable here and a copy of written authority by the principal bestowing authority upon the agent should be requested and attached to the lease agreement.

Although there are situations whereby the agent may bind the principal without express authority, these situations generally involve litigation. It is always wise to secure evidence of written authority in order to avoid misunderstanding.

Partnerships

In general, the signature of one competent partner is sufficient to bind all. However, it is wise to secure the signatures of all the general partners, if possible.

In limited partnerships the total number of partners is usually small and securing the signatures of all general partners should not be difficult.

In many general partnerships with a large number of individuals, several managing partners are frequently appointed in the certificate of partnership. It is usually sufficient to secure the signatures of these managing partners.

These are matters that should be reviewed with a lawyer.

OBTAINING A SPOUSE'S SIGNATURE

When one or more of the parties to a lease agreement are individuals, it is wise to secure the signatures of the spouses (wife or husband) of each. Tenants contracting with an individual will want to protect their present leasehold rights from any community property interest or future interest that might adversely affect them after the owner's death.

Any such difficulties may be avoided by having the spouse of the owner join in the lease agreement.

The owner dealing with an individual tenant has a different concern. The owner will want to make sure the assets of the tenant will remain available as a source of compensation for damages in the event of breach of the lease by the tenant.

In short, the wish is to ensure that the tenant who is transferring assets to a spouse will not defeat these rights. Securing the signature of the individual tenant's spouse avoids this concern.

THE DEPICTION OF THE LEASED PREMISES

The depiction of the leased premises may be in the form of a legal description of the property by address, by an area or size and dimensions relating to a portion of a given property, or an attached floor plan.

Whichever description is used, it must clearly identify the space and specific property being conveyed.

SUPPORTING THE AGREEMENT

To be valid, a contract must be supported by consideration. Consideration is the exchange of something of value. It may be the immediate payment of currency, barter or exchange, or could also be the giving of a promise by one party to perform future acts in return for another promise by the other party.

In the lease situation consideration is most often an exchange of promises. For instance, the owner may promise to deliver use and possession of the property to the tenant for a specified term in return for the tenant's promise to pay the owner a specified rent.

Sometimes there may be an additional consideration, such as an immediate payment of currency in the form of an advance rental or deposit.

The statement of consideration in the lease agreement is contained in the conveyance and payment of the rental clause that includes the amount of rent to be paid, the method of payment, and to whom payment is to be made.

It is advisable to specify in the rental clause the total rent to be paid over the entire lease term. The method of payment should be a specific amount of money whether monthly, quarterly, or annually, as the case may be.

THE USE OF THE PREMISES

In order for a contractual agreement to be legally enforceable it must have legality of purpose. For example, an agreement to pay a sum of money based on the loss of a wager is not a legal purpose in those jurisdictions in which gambling is illegal.

Such an agreement, no matter how well written, is unenforceable due to the illegality of the contract's purpose. For this reason, professional gamblers in these jurisdictions maintain their own private methods of enforcement.

The lease should include the purpose for which the premises are to be used. This clause would include the legal utilization and purpose of the agreement, thereby creating an enforceable contract insofar as the owner/lessor is concerned. A "use" clause is added to prevent damage to the property or an adverse effect on it due to a use other than that for which it was intended.

For example, in an apartment lease, it is customary to state that the leased premises be utilized only as a residence for the tenant's immediate family and for no other purpose. The intent of such a clause is to preclude its use as, for example, a business centre or dance hall. This would infringe upon the rights of other tenants, damaging the property's image and desirability as a residential building.

It is further designed to preclude overcrowding of the premises by permitting the tenant to house an unreasonable number of people in the apartment. Overcrowding can result in physical damage to the space, as well as, create noise and health problems adversely affecting the property, its status and its value in the marketplace.

EXPIRATION DATES

A clear statement relating to commencement and expiration dates must be included within the lease agreement as matters of common sense and general legality.

Without the inclusion of such a statement the terms of the leasehold would be so vague as to be unenforceable. In addition, a lease with no stated term may violate statutory or common law, such as the Rules Against Perpetuities, in some jurisdictions.

THE RIGHTS AND OBLIGATIONS OF THE PARTIES

The statement of the rights and obligations of the parties to the lease specifies a number of points, such as who is responsible for:

- repairing the damaged interior of the premises
- maintaining the roof
- repairing damaged plumbing facilities
- replacing broken glass

A whole series of time-honoured clauses have become almost standard provisions of any lease. These clauses shall be considered in detail, with emphasis on the reasons for their inclusion and the specific language that has been used as they have acquired specific legal meaning. Many are clauses utilized only in special situations that have grown as the world of commerce and the economy have become more sophisticated and complex.

COVENANTS (PLEDGES OR PROMISES)

A lease essentially breaks into three different types of covenants:

- tenant's covenants
- landlord's covenants
- mutual covenants

REGULAR OR STANDARD LEASE COVENANTS

Payment of Rent

This is the statement of consideration in the lease agreement and is contained in the conveyance and payment of rental clause in which the amount of the rental to be paid, the method of payment and to whom the payment is to be made, are covered.

It is advisable to specify in the rental clause the total rent to be paid over the entire lease term. The method of payment should be an amount of dollars monthly, quarterly or annually as the case may be.

Quiet Enjoyment

This clause began in early English land law. It states that the tenant is granted quiet, peaceful, and sole enjoyment of the leased premises without unwarranted interference by the lessor or anyone acting on behalf of the lessor.

Maintenance

This clause is intended to clearly state which of the parties is to be responsible for specific maintenance of the property. The amount of the rent will determine which of the parties will assume the expense of maintenance.

Generally, in residential apartments, only the owner/lessor bears the responsibility for damage to the property over and above normal wear and tear.

In the apartment lease, the assumption of responsibility for maintenance by the lessor is often not made explicit but is implied by the omission of any provision casting responsibility upon the tenant.

In other words, if the agreement is silent, the implication is that the landlord – who usually prepares the lease form – bears the responsibility.

In comparison, in the commercial or store lease, it is the general rule that responsibility for all maintenance of the property shall rest on the tenant, with the exception of repairs to the roof or other structural components.

Office buildings may be a different story. Usually, the landlord is accountable for the maintenance (including providing a janitor and decorator) of the public space. Maintenance liability for areas leased exclusively for tenant use varies. In any case, language is used with the clear intent to place responsibility.

Compliance with Code or Law

This clause places accountability for any expense to provide facilities required by any ordinance or code. The clause usually only appears in commercial leases and usually provides that meeting such requirements shall be the responsibility of the tenant, as rental levels were established based on the landlord's capital investment at the time of commencement.

Utilities

This clause simply states which utilities will be supplied at the expense of the landlord and which of them the tenant must pay.

Insurance Clauses

Insurance clauses are found most often in commercial and office building leases. They are essentially directed at three separate problems.

The first is the use to which a tenant may put the property, since such use may amplify the risk of loss on the part of the insurance arbiter, resulting in an increase in insurance rates and cost. The insurance use provision is designed to place accountability on the tenant for such excess cost.

A second insurance clause requires the tenant to carry liability insurance. This protects the owner from any expense resulting from any injury to a third party on the premises.

The "hold harmless" clause may afford the landlord some protection in such a case. However, additional protection may be secured by requiring the tenant to carry liability insurance of a certain minimal amount, thus ensuring that there will be a fund (provided at the tenant's expense in premiums) against which an injured party may recover.

Often this clause necessitates that the landlord and agent be named as additional insurances on the policy. This clause does not, however, remove the necessity for landlords to carry their own liability policy.

A third insurance provision is the "insurance escalator" clause. Although it is not frequently seen, the clause acknowledges that rental rates are in part predicated upon current insurance rates and that the tenant on a pro-rated annual basis will support any increase in rates.

Where insurance expense is included within an operating cost escalator clause, no additional special clause is required.

Improvements and Alterations

A standard provision in most leases is a clause that forbids the tenant from making any alterations or improvements without the express permission of the landlord. The utilization of the clause has several purposes:

- to avert any structural damage to the property by ensuring that plans provide for proper installation
- to evade the possibility of liens being filed against the property, in the event that contractors are not paid, by requiring the tenant to file and post notices of non-responsibility by the landlord with all contractors
- to allow the landlord the opportunity to analyze what consequence the improvements might have upon real estate tax assessed against the property and to permit negotiation for additional rental because of such increases (this is particularly important in the absence of a tax escalator clause or a clause requiring the tenant to pay all taxes)
- to ensure that the proposed improvements are in harmony with the best interests of the property and will not negatively affect value

Assignment or Subletting

In most leases it is standard to include a provision that prohibits the tenant from permitting another party to occupy all, or part of the leased premises, through an assignment of the lease or by subletting without the written consent of the landlord.

This clause can have several different purposes, depending on whether the lease is an apartment, office, or commercial lease.

The Apartment Lease

In the apartment lease, residence has been granted to a specific tenant who the landlord deems will be financially responsible and will occupy the unit in relative harmony with the other tenants.

The landlord does not wish to give up his right to choose compatible and financially solvent tenants by allowing a free assignment of the premises. This clause preserves the landlord's right to choose tenants, although in most apartment leases the landlord will not withhold consent to an assignment or subleasing unreasonably.

The clause also prevents the occupancy of a unit by more than the maximum number of individuals as established by the landlord's policy. In many areas of Canada, the landlord's rights of approval have been modified or curtailed by legislation, resulting in a situation where such approval may not be unfairly withheld.

Commercial and Office Leases

The assignment provision has even more bearing in commercial and office leases. The rate of rent recognized in the lease has been based on the financial accountability of the specific tenant and the particular use to which the tenant intends to put the property, which is assumed to be its best and highest use.

Often the use of the property will affect the surrounding property that is owned by the landlord (i.e. a shopping centre).

The free replacement of an assignee or sub lessee might affect the value of the leased property in a negative fashion and definitely represents a changed condition of use that may dictate a different rental policy or structure.

It is crucial to note that a subletting or assignment of the leased premises by the original tenant does not completely absolve the original tenant their responsibility under the lease. Unless released through documentation by the landlord, the initial tenant remains liable for the faithful performance of the lease in possible event of breach by the sub lessee or assignee.

Partial Destruction

The rationale behind the "partial destruction" clause is to prevent termination of the lease by the tenant by reason of a partial or total destruction of the leased premises in the event of fire or other mishap.

It declares the procedures and rights that would be applied in the event of such circumstances. Without this clause the landlord could be charged with violation of the lease if the premises became uninhabitable after such events as:

- a fire
- a flood
- any other mishap which might have damaged the property

Most such clauses specifically assert that the lease will not be terminated due to a potential event of a partial destruction, provided that the landlord makes repairs within a specific duration of time.

The landlord must decrease rents for the period that the premises are under repair with no liability above and beyond that to the tenant. Many destruction clauses also provide that if damages surpass a certain percentage of the total, the landlord retains the option of either repairing the premises within a specific duration of time or concluding the lease without any accountability for any damages to the tenant.

Should total destruction occur, the lease is generally terminated.

Default

The function of the "default" clause is to create procedures and rights in the event of default by either of the parties to the lease agreement.

The default clause often provides the landlord with the right to instant re-entry and repossession of the premises in the event of default by the tenant. Under this clause, the landlord may remove the tenant's property and instantly re-rent the property in order to minimize any potential losses.

The default clause often provides that – upon the event of default – the entire rent balance for the remaining term becomes due and payable. If it is allowable under community law, the landlord may immediately sue for a specific sum. He/she may be obliged to alleviate the loss by seeking a release of the premises as soon as possible.

When permitted by local law, the default clause also allows the landlord to take possession of the tenant's property located on the premises as security for any loss suffered.

A supplementary provision that is often incorporated is the allocation of accountability for legal fees to the defaulting party.

Please note: the law of the jurisdiction, either provincial or municipal, frequently controls the rights of the landlord in the event of breach of the lease or default. Therefore you may deem it crucial to have a lawyer who is familiar with the law of the local area review and approve the contents of any default clause.

"Hold Harmless"

Another standard stipulation is the "hold harmless" clause. It provides that the landlord will not be liable to the tenant or any third party for damages or injury incurred in, on or about the leased premises.

The tenant agrees to hold the landlord harmless (indemnified against loss) against any claims of liability against the landlord.

This clause is of great importance in commercial leases where the accountability for virtually all maintenance rests with the tenant and is above and beyond the landlord's surveillance and regulation.

The language of the "hold harmless" clause is apt to be all-inclusive, appearing to release landlords from all responsibility, whether or not it is a result of their own fault or negligence. However, general principles of law will somewhat modify this language in the sense that one cannot contract away responsibility for one's own negligence.

In order to determine whether or not negligence has occurred (which is the foundation for negligence), will depend on facts and the law. A jury will decide the result and juries are not known to favour landlords.

Often, suits are brought against landlords, along with, or opposed to, suits brought against tenants. The "hold harmless" clause makes sure that the tenant for any loss for which the landlord may not be primarily responsible indemnifies the landlord.

However, please note that landlords should not depend on the "hold harmless" clause as a replacement for the liability insurance that will take care of their own interests.

Right to Re-Entry

While the "quiet enjoyment" clause gives tenants the entitlement to the exclusive utilization and inhabitation of the leased premises, the "re-entry" clause allows a landlord to re-enter the premises for a specific purpose after its transference has taken place.

The most widespread characteristic of this clause gives the landlord the right to re-enter the premises in order to make inspections (at times which are reasonable for the tenant), make necessary repairs and post notices (generally notices of non-accountability during alterations or improvements by the tenant).

It is the "right of re-entry" clause that affords the landlord the right of the lease. Right to re-entry clauses are also used to set forth procedures to be followed in case of any of these events:

- insolvency
- bankruptcy
- tenant receivership

Holdover Tenants

The "holdover tenant" clause supplies the terms of tenancy when a tenant does not leave the leased premises when his lease has expired. This clause is important because common law provides that if a tenant does not leave the premises when the lease ends, and if immediate action is not taken by the landlord, the tenant could renew the lease for a period of time covered by one rental instalment.

Therefore, in regards to those cases in which rent is paid annually (as may be the case with leases), the lease is extended for a period of one full year, often to the disappointment of both landlord and tenant.

Many holdover clauses provide that, in the event the occupancy extends beyond the expiration of the lease term, the tenant shall continue the same terms and conditions on a month-to-month basis. This provides a reasonable amount of time for either action or lodging for either party.

Please note: the holdover tenancy clause should not be mistaken for the "delivery of possession" or "automatic renewal" clauses, which will be explained in upcoming sections – each of which was created to serve an entirely different purpose.

Delivery of Possession

The rationale of this clause is to eliminate any loss to the landlord by reason of inability to allow possession of the premises on the agreed date.

It is sometimes the case that the inability to deliver may be due to the holding-over of occupancy by the previous tenant, or it may result from the fact that the landlord has not completed work required to deliver the premises in the agreed condition.

In such cases, the landlord is prohibited from conveying the possession and use of the property on the agreed date. This is technically a breach of the lease. The "delivery" clause prevents a voiding or termination of the lease agreement and eliminates or alleviates any loss that the landlord might otherwise experience.

The majority of delivery clauses only prohibit voiding of the lease or abatement of rent during the period the premises are unavailable. Some require that possession must be afforded the new tenant within a specified time or the lease becomes voidable at the tenant's option.

The clause becomes very crucial when the lease agreement covers premises which are to be built for the tenant. In these leases, some damages may be provided to the new tenant, either as liquidated damages or in the form of a penalty to the landlord.

Sign Restriction

Most commercial leases forbid the creation or affixation of any signs without the owner's written consent. The reasons for the stipulation are as follows:

- to make certain that the proposed sign will be affixed to the building in a manner which will not injure the structure
- to make certain that the sign is consistent with the personality of

- the building and its surroundings – this is especially significant in the case of neighbourhood and regional shopping centres
- to make certain that the sign is erected at the tenant's expense and without landlord responsibility regarding liens or other claims

Many sign restrictions clauses will also require conformity to local codes and regulations. Furthermore, many such clauses state that, once fastened, the sign becomes part of the property and may not be removed by the tenant at the expiration of tenancy or without the landlord's consent in case of replacement.

Bankruptcy or Insolvency

The bankruptcy and insolvency clauses confirm procedure to be followed and rights of the landlord in the event of tenant bankruptcy or insolvency, or the appointment of a receiver.

The rights of the landlord in these cases are regulated by the bankruptcy laws applicable in the case and could involve provincial and/or federal law.

The preparation of these clauses should necessitate the involvement of a lawyer who is familiar with the laws applicable.

All bankruptcy and solvency clauses usually provide that an act of bankruptcy or insolvency on behalf of the tenant shall be equivalent to a breach of the lease. All rents owing under the full term of the lease become due immediately.

Rights of re-entry are also usually allowed, including the right to remove all of the tenant's property and to immediately re-lease the premises, without jeopardy to any claims for loss the landlord may have against the bankrupt tenant.

Time is of the Essence

As long as the requirements of a contract are performed within a reasonable amount of time as specified in the contract, there is no breach of the contract.

However, by including the axiom "time is of the essence," performance of the contract requirements is to be at the very moment explicitly specified in the contract. Otherwise, the contract has been breached and one of the parties would have the opportunity to claim for damages.

Therefore, rent that is paid on the second day of the month—rather than on the first – would amount to a breach of contract on the tenant's behalf, enabling the landlord to terminate the lease and claim damages.

While such a clause might be advantageous to a landlord in a rapidly rising market, it can also be a fairly dangerous one.

By and large, it is believed that there is no positive reason for the inclusion of a "time is of the essence" stipulation in a lease agreement because all problems of reference here relate to performance of conditions and obligations, and are thus dependent on a continuing relationship between the tenant and owner.

Condemnation

Form leases in the past did not usually include the "condemnation clause." But in more recent times the condemnation clause has become important in any community.

During the past 25 years, governments (federal, provincial, municipal, and quasi-governmental authorities) have taken a great deal of private property through condemnation or expropriation proceedings for urban renewal, construction of major thoroughfares and throughways.

If the government is to take property during the term of lease, the landlord is prohibited from performing the balance of the agreement.

In the absence of a condemnation clause, inability to perform constitutes a breach of the lease agreement and renders the landlord liable to the tenant for possible damages. Although the landlord receives compensation for the taking of the property in a condemnation award, the potential liability represents an entirely separate proceeding.

Where a condemnation clause was not utilized, it was common for the award to the tenant to be a disproportionately large amount compared to the award received by the landlord.

The function of this clause is to successfully eliminate any sharing with the tenant of an award received in condemnation or expropriation proceedings. The clause also eliminates any liability to the tenant due to the landlord's inability to perform the agreement because of condemnation.

Upon condemnation, the lease agreement immediately terminates, with all further rights and obligations ceasing. The tenant has no right to receive any compensation from the landlord because of such termination.

The clause also expressly states that the tenant shall have no right to receive any part of any award received by the landlord in condemnation proceedings unless otherwise authorized by government or court.

Automatic Renewal

Short-term leases often provide for lease renewal upon the same terms and for the same period of time.

The primary advantage of this clause is that is does away with the need for renewal negotiation on short-term leases, especially in those cases where occupancy for more than the initial term is likely.

The notice period provided is generally long enough to allow for negotiation with the tenant for a renewal, if it is desired, or to secure a quick replacement.

When the automatic renewal clause is used, some care is needed if the rent is to be raised. The landlord's agent must alert the tenant in a timely manner, letting him/her know that the current lease will be terminated at its expiration and advising that a new lease may be secured at the increased rent. Otherwise, the automatic renewal clause will take effect and the new rent cannot be put into operation until the renewal period has terminated, assuming that proper notice has been given.

The clause may also apply to short-term commercial leases, especially in strip-store locations where the likelihood of increased rentals in the future is small and where long-term leases prove unmarketable.

Service of Notice

Practically all leases, regardless of whether they are residential, commercial or office buildings, include this clause. Under this clause, the tenant waives the right to notice for actions resulting from non-payment of rent or other violations during the occupancy of the space.

In the various provinces these notices are called by different names:

- "5-day notices"

- "10-day notices"
- "notice to quit"
- "notice to terminate tenancy"
- "dispossessory"

These notices governed by local statutes afford some protection and a procedure for the tenant to follow. In most provinces a tenant may contract to waive the right to these notices, thereby saving time and reducing the chance of error in providing notices.

Waiver of Notice

A party may not waive the right to money judgments and the waiver notice would be null and void when used in these situations. The landlord whose lease contains a waiver of notice can annul the effect of such a waiver by routinely issuing notices to the tenant.

For example, if a lease provides a waiver of notice such as a 10-day notice for the payment of rent and the landlord issues 10-day notices as a threat or reminder notice, the landlord then, in effect, waives the waiver and may not proceed with an action without issuing a 5-day notice.

CONTENTS OF A LEASE

From province to province the precise and legal requirements of the lease will vary, so landlords should be sure to check with their lawyer or apartment association for the local laws in their area.

For free information on the subject, contact your provincial government. They usually possess publications that outline the specific laws in your area. As with the offer to purchase, you can use the pre-printed legal lease forms that are available at any stationery store.

A typical lease should cover all of these fundamental points:

1) The name and address of both parties

2) The date of the agreement
3) A description of the dwelling, including:

   a) unit number

b) address
c) number of units in the building
d) the city

A total inventory of the property's condition and any articles in it should be taken when a tenant moves in. (A landlord/tenant inspection inventory is included in this publication.)

Such an inventory provides proof of the original condition, should the property be damaged by the tenant during the duration of his possession. Both parties should sign the inventory.

Photographs may help to support whatever information is contained in the inspection inventory.

4) The term of the agreement, providing the precise starting and ending days of the tenancy.

For annual leases, an automatic renewal clause (see previous section) can be written into the lease in order to avoid writing a new lease each year. But, in these days of rent control, it may prove to be a better idea to have a terminating lease.

With a terminating lease, the monthly payments can be adjusted each year. In a one-year contract the rent must be set for one year. Avoid locking yourself into a fixed rental payment (especially during times of high inflation and/or a landlord's market); you could use a month-to-month lease.

A month-to-month lease runs from one month to the next, renewing automatically at the end of each. Accordingly, the rent can be raised in any month as long as the tenant is given ample notice within the legal limits brought about by rent controls in the area.

In Ontario, ninety days written notice must be provided to the tenant before the rent can be raised.

5) An amount of rent, including when it is due and how it should be paid.

You may choose to include in the rent section of the lease a fee for cleaning the vacated premises into which the new tenant is about to move.

It may be prudent to avoid cleaning the apartment if a tenant is already living there; this way the potential charge can be optional to the new tenant. Some prospective tenants may prefer to avoid the charge and move into a dirty apartment. The cost can be a flat fee of your choosing and should be collected before the new tenant moves in.

6) The name or names of those people who represent the landlord should be supplied to the tenant so that the landlord's duties can be carried out through these individuals

7) The use of the premises. If the premises are to be rented for residential use, make sure a clause is included in the lease that prevents business use.

8) The names of all those who will inhabit the premises, and the total number of all of these individuals.

    The lease should definitely state all parties who will inhabit the residence and should possibly also contain a clause that would cover any potential change in this number.

    Landlords may desire to charge a rent increase if more people are living on the premises than explicitly stated on the lease. If a clause such as this is written into the lease, it should be less trouble than usual to raise rents, even in regions that are covered by rent control.

    It should also be stated here that the individual signing the lease is doing so on behalf of all the other individuals who will inhabit the premises (unless they too are signing the lease). This way the remaining individuals are still covered under the lease even if the individual who signed moves away.

9) Whose responsibility it is to pay the utilities should also be included.

10) The amount of prepaid rent (often referred to as "last month's rent") and the terms of that amount.

11) Last month's rent:
    There are some provinces in which landlords are prohibited from holding a security deposit. However, it is legal for the land-

lord to collect last month's rent, and should any complications arise, that money is in the landlord's hands.

It is worth noting that this amount can only be used for the last month's rent. If any damage disputes occur, the landlord has the right to sue the tenant for reparation, but he is not allowed to use last month's rent to cover any damages.

12) Agreement to obey the provincial and regional laws regarding tenancy. This usually covers such areas as:

   a) landlord and tenant rights
   b) how and when the lease should be terminated
   c) any restrictions on rent raises brought about by rent control

The provincial acts usually cover the tenants' rights in reference to:

   a) repairs
   b) security
   c) renewal
   d) privacy
   e) subletting
   f) access to information regarding the landlord

The provincial acts also cover the landlord's rights with respect to:

   a) evictions
   b) rent in arrears
   c) prepaid rent (last month's rent)
   d) deposits
   e) overstaying tenants

Before strict regulation, most provinces allowed the lease to be decided by mutual agreement between the landlord and the tenant. If something is not covered by a provincial or regional law, the landlord and tenant can add an agreement about that particular aspect to the lease.

But when there is a law in effect, it overrules any agreements made in the lease. For example, a signed lease agreement could have a stipulation that states that a tenant can be evicted without warning.

Because this is against provincial law, the law would triumph and the landlord could not evict the tenant without warning. The law shields a tenant who is not in a position to haggle about the stipulations of a lease upon entering those specific premises.

13) Any special covenants that have been agreed upon by both tenant and landlord should also be included in the lease.

Before incorporating special covenants into the lease, make sure to find out which areas are already covered by the landlord/tenant laws in your province. This will help you to avoid unnecessary duplication.

Some areas you may want to cover by special covenants include:

a) 24 hour notice to enter the premises
b) repairs
c) pets
d) noise
e) subletting
f) tenant absence
g) overstaying
h) option to purchase
i) parking
j) waterbeds
k) prohibited activities
l) balcony cooking
m) laundry
n) signs on windows
o) painting
p) more than one occupant

SPECIAL COVENANTS

It would be prudent to include most, if not all, of the following in the lease.

1) Drains and waste pipes:

   To stop a tenant from clogging drains due to negligence (such as getting rid of grease, or dropping articles), there should be a covenant in the lease to the effect of:
   "All drains and waste pipes were clear when the tenant moved in and therefore any stoppage (either partial or complete) during his tenancy is his responsibility to repair."

2) Pets:

   A fairly large percentage of the population has pets. Any landlord who refuses outright to rent to them is cutting into his market of prospective renters.

   It may be a good idea to allow pets, but to retain a clause in the lease which covers all items with respect to pets.

   You could possibly charge pet owners a higher rate of rent, depending on the type and size of the pet, but make sure to outline the circumstances under which a pet is allowed on the premises, such as:

   a) the size and number of pets
   b) Any restrictions on the kind of pet, such as "domestic pets only" (for example: no llamas, manatees or turkeys)
   c) where on the premises the animal is allowed and/or not allowed

3) Covenant for legal action:

   Landlords should include in the lease a stipulation that the tenant will be liable for any legal costs incurred by the landlord in enforcing the Landlord/Tenant Act.

This should include both court costs and attorney's fees. The lease could also state that the tenant will also be responsible for paying any court costs sustained in enforcing the lease.

4) Covenant for noise:

A one-line clause could be incorporated into the lease preventing noise during a specific period of time. The period would depend on work schedules, and others living in/near the premises.

5) Subletting:

In most provinces, landlords are prohibited from allowing tenants to sublet their apartments. It should be noted that under this law the original tenant remains legally responsible for the new submitted tenants.

If you live in an area where there is no such law in effect, you may want to insert a covenant stating that any new tenants must be approved by the owner before moving into the premises.

6) Abide by the municipal, provincial and federal laws:

Such a stipulation prevents tenants from carrying on any illegal activities within the building, along with providing a means of eviction for criminals.

7) A clause for immediate action:

If any of the lease covenants are violated, legal or other action can be taken right away, without notice. One could also stipulate any exceptions to this.

8) No unauthorized washing machines shall be permitted in the apartment at any time:

This stipulation protects the landlord against unnecessary damage to the plumbing system that could be the result of washing machines being used with improper hook-ups.

9) Any change(s) in this lease:

   Must be in writing and initialled by both the lessor and the lessee.

10) Entry rights of owner:

   In most provinces, unless otherwise written into the lease, the only time that the landlord may enter the tenant's premises is in case of emergency or with the tenant's explicit consent.

   It should be written into the lease that the landlord may enter the premises upon 24 hours notice to the tenant. This would allow the landlord to show the apartment to prospective tenants upon receipt of termination from the current tenant.

   By knowing the laws in your area, you can insert a covenant into the lease agreement to make sure you have all the legal rights available to you.

11) Children's play area:

   If children are permitted on the premises, and the accommodation in question is a building shared by others (such as an apartment building), you might want to insert a covenant which outlines the area(s) where children are not supposed to play, for example:

   a) hallways
   b) lobbies
   c) elevators

   In addition to this, you may also consider adding a stipulation that prohibits tenants from keeping any personal property in the common areas.

12) Partial payment of rent:

In some areas the laws state that once a partial payment of rent has been received by the landlord, all court orders relating to non-payment cease.

In order to prevent this legal loophole you can include in the lease a stipulation to this effect:

"A partial payment of rent by the aforesaid lessee does not, under any circumstances, affect the contents of this lease or any legal notice which is currently active."

13) Garbage disposal:

All refuse should be properly separated and disposed of in the proper areas. Recycling material (this varies, depending on the area) should not be thrown into garbage bins or down garbage chutes.

This stipulation should also cover the type of wrapping to be used for the garbage (i.e. sealed containers or plastic garbage bags to prevent leakage).

14) Balcony cooking:

Include a stipulation forbidding balcony cooking if this practise is not already covered by the covenant to obey municipal, provincial and federal law. In many areas it is illegal to cook on a balcony; therefore, this practise would be covered under Covenant #6.

It would be sensible to examine the lease periodically in order to review any outdated policies or to implement new policies. If the number of residents has changed, or if the person who signed the official lease has moved, you may want to write up a new lease that reflects these developments.

Your lease will help you in selecting tenants. The prospective tenant who balks at or tries to circumvent any of your conditions may turn out to be a problem for you in the future. It would be better to avoid the problem altogether by rejecting the tenants rather than catering to his/her demands.

If you have multiple tenants, such as in the case of an apartment building or multiplex, you will want to remain consistent from tenant to tenant in regards to the policies that you uphold.

Playing favourites is likely to make people unhappy, which will in turn cause you headaches.

Once both parties sign the lease, it is a legally binding contract between the two parties involved.

TERMINATION OF TENANCY AGREEMENT

When signing a lease with a tenant, you should also get him to sign a termination of tenancy agreement. A sample of such an agreement will be provided at the end of this chapter. This contract makes it much easier to evict a tenant when he promises to leave.

This way, if you don't desire to renew the lease with that particular tenant, he is forced to leave. Sometimes it is almost impossible to get the tenant evicted from your premises, even if the lease has run out.

If you want to renew the lease, it is your option as the landlord to ignore the termination contract.

Your tenant should sign a new termination of tenancy contract during their occupancy if they desire to move out at a specific date of their choosing that is earlier than when the lease states they must leave the premises. For example, if the tenant gives you two months' notice, you should have the contract dated for the day that the tenant agreed to leave.

Otherwise, if he changes his mind, it cause problems for you. This is why it is important to have everything in writing.

A termination of tenancy contract is a relatively new legal tool available to protect the landlord. It is not available in all provinces, so check with your local rent review board to see if they have such a contract.

SPECIAL CLAUSES

FOR OFFICE BUILDINGS (COMMERCIAL)

Operating Cost Escalation Clause (Existing Building)

The function of such a clause it to shield the landlord against inflation and rising costs. It is not meant to help the landlord make a profit, but to make sure that at all times the landlord is in the very same position, in terms of costs, as on the initial day when the space was originally leased.

This escalation clause should never be given away. It is better to make compromises when the lease begins (for example, better building standards, or the waiver of rent for a few months) than it is to interfere with future operation of the property.

All tenants should be kept on the same base period. The initial full calendar year of possession by the tenant should be the base year. If the tenant takes occupancy during the early part of a calendar year, then that becomes the base year.

Operating Cost Escalation (New Building)

This stipulation is different from that of an operating building because there is no experience in operating the building and therefore no actual operating expense figures.

Operating costs must thus be specifically defined, and start-up years must be determined as though the building was fully occupied.

Tax Participation

This stipulation is found in the beginning of the lease with an equitable percentage to cover the tenant's share of inevitable tax escalation.

FOR RETAIL AND SHOPPING CENTRES

The Expropriation Clause

This clause is a part of other leases, but not to the extent that it is used for shopping centres. Many of the leases for primary tenants of shopping centres have a clause that provides for cancellation of the lease, in the event that a certain proportion of the shopping centre, or a part of the parking lot, is expropriated.

This clause has become crucial in recent times.

Tax Escalator Clause

The tax escalator clause has been utilized in office building leases and shopping centre leases for a substantial period of time. Consideration is also being given to the use of tax escalators in apartment leases.

Merchant's Association Clause

This clause is unique to the shopping centre lease. The Merchants' Association is made up of a group of varied tenants in the shopping centre. The Association promotes the entire centre and works to develop it as a merchandising entity.

This clause is mandatory in most shopping centre leases.

Percentage Lease

The main concern of a commercial lease is its percentage clause. Many leases have a minimum applied against gross sales over a certain point.

Common Areas

Only a small number of residential leases have a common area clause, but leases of office buildings may have one. This is due to the fact that the common areas in a shopping centre are more definite, relating to the areas that are not under a specific, distinct lease:

- parking areas
- sidewalk areas
- service areas

Exclusive-Use and Radius Restrictions

This clause presides over such aspects of shopping centres as:

- similar-type businesses
- sale of specific items
- category base too broad (i.e. women's wear, national chain stores)

- competing retail outlets

Please note that certain restrictions that apply to areas of the parking lot may also be included in the lease.

Operating Covenants

"Operating covenants" in shopping centres can be of primary importance and may be mandatory requirements from the major anchor tenants.

This clause compels the tenant to continue operation of the business at the location, even if this is proving unprofitable. The impetus behind this obligation on the tenant is to avoid a potential situation wherein a chain might simply closes down a store even though they continue to pay the rent.

This would have a significant effect on other merchants in the centre as a result of reduced traffic, besides the fact that a closed store would not generate a percent rental.

Sublease or Assignment

It is crucial to be aware that even though the two terms "sublease" and "assignment" are often misused or taken to have the same meaning, there is an important technical difference.

The term "sublease" implies that a residual term of at least one day of the lease reverts back to the original tenant. In other words, the sub lessee will have a term that will be at least one whole day less than that remaining under the head lease.

An "assignment" on the other hand is for the entire remaining term without any reversion right to the original tenant. Neither arrangement should be permitted without the specific written consent of the lessor (although it will often be necessary to give the tenant written assurance that "such consent will not be unreasonably withheld.")

Neither assignment nor sublet consent should generally release the original tenant from the obligations under the lease unless this has been specifically negotiated with and agreed to by the landlord.

It is, generally speaking, preferable to attach a landlord's consent as a separate document from the sublease or assignment documentation between the head tenant and the subtenant, so the landlord does not become an unwilling party to the agreement, but remains merely a "consenter."

SAMPLE LEASE AGREEMENTS

The following is a sample of the contents of a residential lease. This lease many not be suitable for all situations and it is advisable to have any legal contract that is being used reviewed by a professional. The purpose of these samples is to further outline the contents and clauses.

RESIDENTIAL LEASE AGREEMENT

1) This lease made this ___ day of _____, 20____ by and between _____ hereinafter called Landlord, and _____ hereinafter called Tenant.

2) **Description:** Witnesseth, the Landlord, in consideration of the rents to be paid and the covenants and agreements to be performed by the Tenant, does hereby lease unto the Tenant the following described premises located thereon situated in the City of _____, and Province of _____.

3) **Terms:** For the term of _____ (months/years) commencing on _____, 20___, and ending on _____, 20___.

4) **Rent:** Tenant shall pay Landlord, as rent for said premises, the sum of $ _____ per month, payable in advance on the first day of each month during the term hereof at Landlord's address above or said other place as Landlord may hereafter designate in writing. Tenant agrees to pay a $ _____ late fee if rent is not paid within 5 days of due date.

5) **Security Deposits:** Landlord herewith acknowledges the receipt of $ _____, which he/she is to retain as security for the faithful performance of the provisions of this lease. If Tenant fails to pay rent, or defaults with respect to any provision of this lease, Landlord may use the security deposit to cure the default or compensate Landlord for all damages sustained by Landlord. Tenant shall immediately on demand reimburse Landlord the sum equal to that portion of security deposit expended by Landlord so as to maintain the security deposit in the sum initially deposited with Landlord. If Tenant performs all obligations under this lease, the security deposit, or that portion thereof that was not previously applied by Landlord, shall be returned to Tenant within 21 days after the expiration of this lease, or after Tenant has vacated the premises.

6) **Possession:** It is understood that if the Tenant shall be unable to enter into and occupy the premises hereby leased at the time above provided, by reason of the said premises not being ready for occupancy, or by reason of holding over of any previous occupant of said premises, the Landlord shall not be liable in damage to the Tenant therefore, but during the period the Tenant shall be able to occupy said premises as hereinbefore provided, the rental therefore shall be abated and the Landlord is to be sole judge as to when the premises are ready for occupancy.

Sample Residential Lease Agreement

7) **Use:** The Tenant agrees that said premises during the term of this lease shall be used and occupied by _____ adults and _____ children, and _____ animals, and for no other purpose whatsoever without the written consent of the Landlord. The Tenant will not use the premises for any purpose in violation of any law, municipal ordinance or regulation, and that on any breach of this agreement the Landlord may at his option terminate this lease and re-enter and repossess the leased premises.

8) **Utilities:** The Tenant will pay for all charges for all water supplied to the premises and shall pay for all gas, heat, electricity, and other services supplied to the premises, except as herein provided.

9) **Repairs and Maintenance:** The Landlord shall at his expense keep and maintain the:

   a. exterior and interior walls

   b. roof

   c. electrical wiring

   d. heating and air conditioning system

   e. water heater

   f. built-in appliances

   g. water lines in good condition and repair

   An exception to this is where damage has been caused by negligence or abuse by the Tenant, in which case the Tenant shall repair same at his sole expense.

   The Tenant hereby agrees that the premises are now in good condition and shall at his own expense maintain the premises and appurtenances in the manner that they were received, reasonable wear and tear excepted.

10) **Alterations and Additions:** The Tenant shall not make any alterations, additions, or improvements to said premises without the Landlord's written consent. All alterations, additions, or improvements made by either of the parties hereto upon the premises, except movable furniture, shall be the property of the Landlord, and shall remain upon and be surrendered with the premises at the termination of this lease.

Sample Residential Lease Agreement

11) **Assignment:** The Tenant will not assign or transfer this lease or hypothecate or mortgage the same or sublet said premises without the written consent of the Landlord.

12) **Default:** If the Tenant shall abandon or vacate said premises before the end of the term of this lease, or if default shall be made by the Tenant in the payment of said rent or any part hereof, or if the Tenant shall fail to perform any of the Tenant's agreements in this lease, then and in each and every instance of such abandonment, vacation, or default, the Tenant's right to enter said premises shall be suspended, and the Landlord may at his option enter said premises, change the locks on the doors of said leased premises, and remove and exclude the Tenant from said premises.

13) **Entry by Landlord:** The Tenant shall allow the Landlord or his agents to enter the premises at all reasonable times and upon reasonable notice for the purpose of inspecting or maintaining the premises, or to show it to prospective tenants or purchasers.

14) **Attorney's Fees:** The Tenant agrees to pay all costs, expenses, and reasonable attorney's fees including obtaining advice of counsel incurred by Landlord in enforcing by legal action or otherwise any of Landlord's rights under this lease or under any law of this province.

15) **Holding Over:** If the Tenant, with the Landlord's consent, remains in possession of the premises after expiration of the term of this lease, such possession will be deemed a month-to-month tenancy at a rental fee equal to the last monthly rental fee, and upon all the provisions of this lease applicable to such a month-to-month tenancy.

The parties hereto have executed this lease on the date first above written.

Landlord: **Tenant:**

By: _____   By: _____

By: _____   By: _____

Sample Residential Lease Agreement

LEASE RENEWAL AGREEMENT

Landlord: _____
Address: _____
Telephone: _____

Property Address/Unit Number:
_____

Resident/Tenant: _____

Lease Expiry Date: _____

Dear _____:

We have enjoyed having you as a tenant. Your current lease expires on _____, 20___. In order to make your lease renewal as early as possible, please take a few minutes to complete this form.

The lease is hereby extended for a period of _____ months, beginning on the first day of _____, 20___, and ending on the last day of _____, 20___.

The following covenants have been added or modified and will become effective with the signing of the lease renewal agreement:

- {Outline additions/modifications here}

<u>For Tenant to Fill Out:</u>

I have read this lease renewal agreement and understand the changes that are being made to my lease:

Date: _____

Signature of Tenant(s): _____

Date: _____

Signature of Landlord(s): _____

Sample Lease Renewal Agreement

AGREEMENT TO TERMINATE A TENANCY

(Landlord's Name), ("Landlord"),
and
(Tenant's Name), ("Tenant"),

Hereby agree to terminate the tenancy with respect to the premises:

(Street Address, Unit Number, City, Province, Postal Code)

On the ____(number) day of _____(month), 20___.

Date: _____

Signature of Tenant(s): _____

Date: _____

Signature of Landlord(s): _____

Sample Agreement to Terminate a Tenancy

Chapter 4:

Property Maintenance

MAINTAINING YOUR RENTAL PROPERTY

This chapter will present the most common requirements for the maintenance and repair of rental properties. Whether one is dealing with a single-family house or a twelve-unit building, many of the repair and maintenance procedures remain the same. Once the principles involved are understood, they can be applied to all of a property manager's rental units.

For this reason, property managers need to learn what to look for and what to expect from their property in its repair and maintenance needs. Then the individual property manager has to decide whether he wishes to do any work by himself and if and when he will hire others to do it for him.

Property managers are responsible for their building's maintenance needs. If they don't have any experience in the maintenance and repair of real estate, this responsibility can be a burden.

If tenants call in the middle of the night to report a broken water pipe or some other crisis, the property manager must know what to do. This could entail several options:

- handling the problem himself,
- relying on a permanent maintenance person, or
- hiring outside professionals

Before encountering such situations, the wise property manager already has a plan in place to deal with them.

Even when there are no emergencies, habitual maintenance will be necessary to keep your rental property in good repair. Ignoring regular maintenance will lead to larger problems, complaints from tenants and, ultimately, will result in less of a profit.

The property manager is responsible for all the scheduling and coordinating of property maintenance, along with the ultimate inspection of the property.

Investors who are new at owning rental properties and property management may be knowledgeable about investing, but may know little about maintenance and repairs. Property maintenance can be one of the most difficult aspects to learn and master when it comes to property management. It can also be the most costly if the rookie property manager does not take steps to learn the trade.

The following sections are areas of the property which merit special attention:

- the exterior property
- the hallways
- the basement
- the roof
- the rental unit interior

INITIAL CONSIDERATIONS

Many landlords who are unable to perform technical work inside their buildings are quite capable of keeping up the exterior. While not everyone may have prior experience with soldering copper pipes or cleaning their heating system, most people are more than qualified to cut grass, or shovel snow.

Still, the question remains – is a property manager's time best spent mowing the lawn or shovelling the driveway? Some landlords don't mind taking care of some or all of the exterior work duties around their properties, as it may give them a chance to take a break from the stress of other related work, not to mention that it can be a good venue for exercise.

It may be more beneficial to hire an individual full-time or part-time (but on a permanent basis) to take care of maintenance duties, or perhaps to hire a company to take care of them. It all depends on the individual property manager and the other responsibilities that he or she has.

Even if a property manager does decide to hire independent contractors to do maintenance and repair work, he still has to be qualified to supervise and coordinate them. When someone is contracted to do a job, they still have to be told:

- what to do
- when to do it
- and, to some extent, how to do it

If a property manager has no idea what the subcontractor should be doing, he is at the subcontractor's mercy. This is not a good position to be in. Try to learn something about a job before you hire people to do it. Read books and research the work until you can speak intelligently about it. Displaying to the contractor that you have a fundamental understanding on the job to be done will help you to avoid being ripped off.

In addition to this, make sure that all of your arrangements and agreements are put down in writing. It is not difficult to become lazy about the required paperwork when working with contractors, but if your property ever has a mechanic's lien placed against it, and if you have to defend your position in court, a written agreement will be essential if you hope to win.

No matter how well you know the contractor, and how trustworthy you deem him to be, don't get careless with your paperwork. You need to write up the Contract and be specific about all the details.

Make sure to allow enough money for maintenance in your operating budget. Due to a lack of experience, many new landlords fail to allot enough to maintaining the property.

It is essential for a property manager to know when to schedule regular maintenance. By watching for early warning signs you can start to prepare for the costs involved in replacing the roof before it begins to leak. Repair bills will get out of hand if you fail to keep the building running smoothly. If you aren't sure exactly what to do or when to do it, don't be afraid to seek help from any of these sources:

- books
- seminars

- and/or consultations with professionals

For example, you could speak to a variety of heating contractors for advice about how often to have your heating system cleaned and tuned up. Don't depend on the advice of just one individual – ask at least three, and then compare their responses. This type of research will help you to avoid many major repairs with simple and regular maintenance.

It is difficult for an inexperienced individual to look at a water heater and to know if it is going to have to be replaced within the next year. This sort of problem can be resolved by having a professional inspection done.

There are companies out there that are dedicated to inspecting and evaluating the condition of buildings. These companies usually provide a detailed report that covers everything – from the roof right down to the foundation. By investing a few hundred dollars for a thorough and professional inspection you have a strong basis for setting your maintenance and repair budget. It may not be fun to find out that your roof will need to be replaced within the next few years, but it is better to know about it well beforehand rather than to wait until you can actually see holes in the roof.

Let's take a virtual tour through the average rental property and see what aspects of its upkeep you will probably encounter.

ASPECTS OF A RENTAL PROPERTY

THE GROUNDS

The grounds of a property entail all of its exterior features that are not actually part of the building itself. These features can include the:

- lawn
- landscaping
- drainage
- parking area
- driveways and parking areas
- sidewalks
- security lights

Depending on the specifications of your rental policy, the following features may also fall into this category:

- garbage disposal
- snow removal
- other exterior services

Making sure that the exterior of your property is in good repair improves its appearance, value, and performance. A tidy and clean exterior will attract more tenants, and these tenants will usually be of a better quality than those who choose to live in neglected properties.

In addition to this, existing tenants will remain happier when they come home to a pleasant rental unit. Tenants rarely enjoy coming home to a building where garbage is strewn across the lawn, not to mention what that would attract. Neglecting lawn care may cause some tenants to assume that it is ok to not take care of their rental unit.

A well-kept building will be more likely to impress a property appraiser than will a rundown one. Your interest in your property will be reflected in a higher appraisal value, which will eventually equate to a large profit. These factors should be motivation enough for you to make sure your lawns and grounds are especially well maintained.

The Lawn, Shrubbery, and Trees

Do not underestimate the effect that a property's lawn – assuming it has one – will have on people, especially the tenants of the building. An unkempt and shaggy lawn is not beneficial in regards to keeping a good relationship with your tenants.

This is why you should keep the grass cut and the leaves raked. A well-manicured lawn goes a long way to making a positive impression on all who will set eyes on your exquisite property.

If your rental property has landscaping, work to keep it looking as good as possible. Make sure to trim hedges and foundation shrubs to keep them below your first-floor windows. If the building looks swamped by wild bushes, people will not want to live in it. Dense greenery can also contribute to crime – if your shrubs are too tall and bushy, deviously sneaky criminals and vandals can effectively hide behind them as virtual shields.

Dead Trees

Until they fall, dead trees often go unnoticed. But when they fall, they can land on your building, a tenant's car, or even on a tenant's head.

Obviously, this can cause excessive damage with potentially expensive (or fatal) consequences. Inspecting the trees and limbs around your property could mean the difference between life and death.

Whenever you detect the possibility of a perilous and harmful situation on your property, don't wait to fix it – act rapidly to steer clear of damages and/or injuries. You may want to call a professional to take care of the situation.

Drainage

Drainage issues in your yard can cause unhappy feelings for your tenants and problems for your building. No one desires to wade through puddles of standing water to get to the door. Standing water in the lawn is not good – the puddles are a terrible nuisance to walk around, and they will draw insects.

If drainage problems occur near the foundation of the building, they can create other problems:

- the basement could flood
- mould could grow in a crawlspace and cause health problems
- the moisture from poor drainage could make the paint peel off the building
- in some cases, damage the foundation

If you have drainage problems, you must make a serious effort to resolve them immediately.

Driveways and Parking Areas

Your building's tenants utilize its driveways and parking areas every day. If these areas were allowed to fall into disrepair, the tenants would become unhappy, and the longer you would allow them to go unattended, the higher would be the cost of eventual repairs.

For example, if your paved driveway already has cracks or holes in it, winter freezing can enlarge them. Insufficient gravel will lead to erosion in graveled driveways. In either case, repairing the driving surface would cost a great deal more than simple maintenance. By sealing paved areas and resurfacing gravelled areas you can preserve your investment without costly repairs.

Security Lights

Tenants are apt to feel more comfortable when their property has security lights. If you already have such lights on your property, take care to keep them in working order.

Burned-out bulbs will make your tenants feel less safe and will encourage criminal activity.

With impact-resistant covers you can protect your lights from rocks. If vandals and children know they can't break the lights (due to the covers), they won't bother to throw rocks at them, and by discouraging the throwing of rocks, you will be able to reduce the number of broken windows in your building.

Garbage Control and Removal

Garbage strewn around your building is unhealthy and ugly. Make sure that the leases being signed by the tenants hold them responsible for their own trash, and if necessary, provide metal containers for their use.

Placing the garbage cans in an enclosed area will shield them from view. If you anticipate that theft or vandalism will be a problem, you can issue each tenant a key for access to the enclosure.

Snow and Ice Removal

Snow removal is a part of every property manager's duties in cold climates. If you anticipate that you will receive snow in the winter, make prior arrangement for its removal – in the autumn is the perfect time.

Getting rid of snow can equate directly to profit:

- tenants who cannot get their cars out of the parking lot cannot get to work

- tenants who cannot get to work cannot pay their rent

It is absolutely in your best interest to provide quick and competent snow removal.

You may be in danger of a potential lawsuit if you leave your exterior walkways and steps covered in ice. Someone could slip, fall on the ice and sustain an injury. This could place you in severe financial trouble, especially in our contemporary culture, where people are apt to sue about anything.

Before it becomes a problem, make arrangements to clear ice away. In the final analysis, you may prefer the minute investment of sand or other ice-removing chemicals to the possibly exorbitant cost of a lengthy legal battle.

EXTERIOR MAINTENANCE

The exterior of your building is exposed to inclement weather, which can definitely deteriorate its overall condition.

To safeguard against significant damage from the elements, you must be willing to provide exterior maintenance. This maintenance may encompass any of the following items:

- the roof and chimney
- siding
- paint
- trim
- doors
- windows
- porches
- other similar items

The Roof and Chimney

If you neglect the building's roof, tenants will notice, and odds are they won't be thrilled by this new development, not to mention that your property will be damaged, thereby lowering it's value.

Water damage from a roof that is leaking can do serious structural harm that can progress to dangerous levels before you even know it exists. If your attic is heavily insulated, it can take months for the water to stain ceilings, but in the meantime you could have rafters rotting or water entering electrical boxes.

Different factors that may affect a roof's lifespan include exposure to extreme heat, which can reduce its useful years, and the type of roofing used.

The novice property manager's untrained eye may not be able to tell if a roof is bad or not. It should be inspected by a professional, who will be able to outline how long it can be expected to last and why.

When it comes time to repair or replace your roof, don't procrastinate.

If your building has a chimney, make sure that it is also receiving its fair share of attention. The mortar joints on the masonry work may occasionally need to be pointed up and the flashing around the chimney should be inspected periodically for leaks.

Depending on the specific type of device that is connected to it, the chimney should be cleaned either annually or on another regular basis.

The Siding and Exterior Trim

If siding and trim are not properly maintained, they will rot. When this happens, it may not be possible to match the existing materials with new ones. This will result in either a non-aesthetically pleasing building, or a great expense to replace more siding and/or trim than is really necessary.

You can detect problems in their early stages by inspecting your siding and trim at habitual intervals. Simple repairs can be made if you detect rot early. A strong paint job is one vital factor in the preservation of your siding and trim.

Another way to ensure a long lifespan is to make sure you have the proper flashing, caulking, and weather protection.

Vinyl or aluminium siding may need to be washed periodically to remove mould and mildew build-up. A good scrub with a power-wash machine will get the job done. Check the Yellow Pages for a contractor who specializes in power washing.

The life of your paint job can be shortened by moisture that collects around your exterior walls, near the foundation. If you have a habitual problem with cracking and peeling paint, check for high moisture content.

A severe problem may mean the wood in your exterior walls and plates is rotting. Keeping your paint in good shape will help to protect your investment while making it more attractive.

Outside Windows and Doors

Outside windows and doors that are not up to par can cost you a lot of money. If you are responsible for heating and cooling your building, they can drain your bank account, especially in older buildings.

Along with the potential for causing energy losses, windows and doors are top contenders for rotting wood. The exterior trim around them will rot quickly if it is not protected. Then the water gathering in windows will work its way into your walls.

Door jams and trim can also fall prey to rot. It is important that all these surfaces be properly caulked and painted.

Porches, Balconies, and Rails

Some landlords forget about porches and rails, but this is a big mistake. If a porch or railing is in bad shape, it could give way and a terrible injury could result. Someone could fall off a high balcony and plunge to their death, which would not be good for you or them.

The same could happen with an injury or death due to faulty porch flooring.

Older buildings are especially prone to bad porches, balconies, and rails, but many landlords prefer to look the other way instead of replacing or repairing them.

While hundreds of thousands of landlords may happily get away with their shaky rails and porches, you will probably not be so lucky. There is no reason to jeopardize the health of your tenants and the wealth of your assets by ignoring a possibly dangerous situation.

Inspect your railings, porches, and balconies. This can't be emphasized enough. If your railings, porches or balconies need repair or replacement, have the job done.

If these structures are in excellent shape, keep them that way. Routine maintenance with paint and frequent inspections can prevent the need for large sums of money spent on replacements. They can also reduce the risks of lawsuits and injuries.

Fire Escapes

Make sure that your building has a fire escape, if it is required to have one. Make sure that it is in top working order. Test it yourself. Don't wait until human lives are in danger to discover that your fire escape doesn't work at all. If a fire inspector finds fault with your fire escape, you may be facing a heavy fine.

INTERIOR COMMON AREAS

Common areas are those areas that are shared by a building's tenants. Some examples of common areas are:

- hallways and security doors
- the basement and the laundry room
- the attic and the crawl space

Common areas are often used on a daily basis, and are the most likely part of the interior of your building to suffer from vandalism.

Hallways and Security Doors

If you don't equip your building with a security door, anyone will be able to wander in. Whereas some may be homeless people who are doing whatever they can to get away from the bone-gnawing cold, others may only be there to steal and vandalize whatever they can.

It is possible that the halls in your building will take a lot of abuse. The hall walls could be damaged when people move furniture in and out of the building, and the floors could be subjected to heavy use in all kinds of weather and particularly suffer from water and melting snow.

Be sure to inspect your halls frequently. You can test the lights to see if they work or not. Test the smoke detectors to see that they are operating properly. All of your tenants will be affected by the condition of your common areas. Few of them will be pleased about missing or burned-out light bulbs or stolen smoke detectors or fire extinguishers.

Nor will they be pleased with junk mail on the floor or bags of smelly garbage left sitting in the hall, attracting rats. If you are able to identify the guilty individual, be adamant that he/she doesn't dirty your halls again. Make sure to keep your halls well lighted and free of clutter. When the code enforcement officer pays your building a visit, the hallways will be one of the first areas he/she looks at.

The potential for all of these problems is omnipresent in multifamily rentals. You can eliminate some of them by installing a security door. You might also consider installing security cameras. By restricting access to the building to authorized tenants, you reduce many maintenance headaches.

After installing security doors, you can look to your tenants when problems occur in the common areas. This is not to say that an outsider couldn't be responsible for the trouble, but the odds are greatly reduced when good security doors are installed.

None of your tenants would especially enjoy leaving their apartments only to trip over a vagrant sleeping in the hallway.

They will be pleased by the security doors, and will be more at ease. With good exterior lighting and security measures in place, you can attract tenants who might have gone to another building if yours had not been so well-equipped.

The Basement and the Laundry Room

Many landlords use the basement of their building as a common area, housing a laundry room or storage facilities. If it is not used this way, it should be locked to prevent prowling tenants from entering.

There are usually many ways for people to get hurt in basements. By restricting access, you reduce your chance of a lawsuit.

If you decide to use the basement as a common area, make sure that it is appropriate for such use. The stairs must be sturdy and equipped with a railing, and both stairs and basement must be adequately lighted.

Install partition walls to limit access to the intended common area. All of your mechanical equipment and non-common areas should be behind locked doors to prevent unauthorized entry.

Some basements are equipped with sump pumps that remove water below the basement floor. If the pump fails, there is a possibility that the basement could flood, so be sure to check the pump monthly in order to diminish that risk.

Laundry rooms that are open to your tenants are a possible trouble area. If the tenants misuse the equipment, the repair bills can pile up rapidly.

Inspect your laundry equipment on a regular basis. If you find a washer or dryer that is not working, be sure to repair it. A tenant who becomes frustrated with a broken machine may abuse it. By keeping your equipment in working condition, you lower your tenants' stress levels.

Inspect the hoses on your washing machines often. Those can become worn and break, and when that happens, unless the valve controlling the water to the hose is cut off, it will release a steady stream of water. Regular inspections of the hoses can reduce the chance of an unwanted flood. If the hoses appear cracked or tender, replace them.

The Attic and the Crawl Space

You probably don't venture into your building's crawl space or attic very often. For that very reason, you should make a concerted effort to inspect your crawl space or attic occasionally.

There should be little need for maintenance in your building's attic, but still, there are a few things you should check for from time to time, such as, roof leaks and/or insect damage. If the roof plywood has turned black, you more than likely have a moisture problem. Small piles of sawdust in the attic may indicate an insect infestation.

Wood-eating insects can destroy your building, so arrange for a professional pest inspection at least once a year. Such inspections are often done without charge, or for a nominal amount.

While you are in the attic, check to see that it is ventilated. A healthy attic needs proper ventilation. There should be:

- gable vents,
- soffit vents, or
- a ridge vent to circulate air

If you have a crawl space foundation, inspect it at least twice a year. Look for standing water, which can cause mould, mildew, rot, and peeling paint.

Insect activity can also be a problem in the crawl space. When you arrange your annual pest inspection, the inspector will check there, as well as, in the attic.

Most crawl space foundations are equipped with air vents mounted in the walls. It is important for the crawl space to receive proper ventilation because cold air blowing on any plumbing pipes there can freeze them.

Protect your pipes from drafts. Insulation or even a heat pipe may be necessary to prevent frozen plumbing.

INSIDE THE RENTAL UNIT

Most routine maintenance will be required inside your rental units. This is where your tenants live and spend their time, therefore where problems are most likely to occur. This includes the heating/cooling system, walls and ceilings, floors and doors. In particular, important consideration must be given to:

- the plumbing system
- the electrical system
- appliances

<u>**The Plumbing System**</u>

The most likely cause of flustered calls from your tenants to you, the landlord, will be problems with the plumbing. If you plan to manage your own property, be prepared for problems ranging from dripping faucets to flooding toilets. One way to play it safe is to learn basic plumbing skills. Since some of the calls will be emergencies, you should either be prepared to play plumber yourself or if you are just not handy find a regular plumber you can depend on and keep him within easy reach.

Plumbers can be an independent bunch. They are expensive and often busy, so plan ahead. Try to establish a relationship with a dependable plumber before you need one. If you wait until you need a plumber to find one, you may not be able to.

Plumbing emergencies know no boundaries. They may occur in the middle of the night or on a weekend. If you need a plumber after normal business hours, you can expect a big bill.

If you have numerous rental units, you may not have as much trouble finding and keeping a plumber. When you give them steady business, plumbers will be likely to respond to your calls.

Many landlords have lease stipulations that hold the tenant responsible for plumbing problems he/she creates, the same as being responsible for something like breaking a window.

By including the proper language in your lease, you can reduce your out-of-pocket expenses on plumbing calls.

However, the routine maintenance of a unit's plumbing is definitely your responsibility. If the toilet's flush valve is bad, causing the toilet to run constantly, repair or replace it. If you are paying the water bill, you will see a noticeable increase in it from all of the wasted water.

The same is true for dripping faucets. It is a good idea to inspect a unit's plumbing at least twice a year. Tenants may not care if their bathtub faucet is dripping, but your water bill will force you to pay the price for the drip.

Include a clause in your lease that will allow you to inspect the interior plumbing on a regular basis.

The Electrical System

While a poor plumbing system can be messy and costly, a faulty wiring system can be deadly and even fatal. Inspect a rental unit's electrical system at the same time that you inspect the plumbing. If the unit has its own fuse panel, check the fuses to see that they are the proper size.

A tenant trying to fix a blown fuse may replace it with one that is wrong for the circuit, and an oversized fuse could lead to a fire. Make stipulations in your lease to prevent tenants from creating electrical safety hazards. If you see extension cords running all over the unit, insist that they be removed.

Appliances

Any electrical appliances you supply should be inspected as warranted. Keep them in good working order to avoid expensive repair bills or premature replacement.

Other Interior Maintenance

Windows and doors that stick may annoy your tenants. Doorbells that don't work are also nuisances, and cabinet or pull out drawers that stick can be really frustrating for anyone.

These may seem like little things but they can all add up to make a tenant very hostile. By going through your units on a regular basis, you can control the small complaints.

Make up "maintenance required" sheets to be filled out by the tenants and have them readily available.

WORKING WITH INDEPENDENT CONTRACTORS

Often landlords retain independent contractors to perform at least some part of their property maintenance; many of them subcontract all of their maintenance and repair work. Independent contractors are often the most cost-effective way to handle building maintenance. Given wages, taxes, and employee benefits, it rarely pays to keep a maintenance person on the payroll.

When arrangements are made for independent contractors to do your work, you are technically the general contractor. If your property is being managed by a professional management firm, they act as the general contractor and probably charge extra for their services.

Many landlords resent these additional charges, but once you start doing your own general contracting, you will understand why management companies have them. It is not easy to be a general contractor. First of all, you must find reputable subcontractors, and after you find them, you must learn to control them. A general contractor must be:

- well-organized
- firm
- in control
- confident

These qualities are not always easy to come by, especially when you have a burly plumber staring you down. Subcontractors can be quite intimidating if you are a general contracting novice. The general contractor assumes final responsibility for the subcontractor's work. If he fails to perform, it is up to you to enforce your rules.

To stay in control, you need strong written agreements. With them, you may still have some disputes, but without them, you will probably have many. A written agreement gives you some power over your subcontractors. They have lien rights and may not hesitate to take you to court. If you can settle your disputes out of court you are money ahead.

Now we'll look more closely at how you should prepare for working with subcontractors.

FINDING YOUR SUBCONTRACTORS

It isn't difficult to find the names and numbers of subcontractors – but it may be difficult to find good and dependable ones.

Few individuals advertise that they are incompetent and unreliable, so you should consider advertisements only as a place to start, not the end of your search. After producing a list of potential subcontractors, you must then qualify them and weed out the bad ones.

Coming across subcontractors via referrals makes your job much less complicated and painless. If a colleague or friend has had good luck with a particular subcontractor then it stands to reason that you can expect similar results.

Look for all your subcontractors before you need them, as the best are most likely to retain regular customers who keep them busy. Check the references they supply, and check with any agency that would have knowledge of legitimate complaints lodged by customers. Do enough homework to reduce your risk of getting less than you expect from your subcontractors.

THE CONTRACTOR'S PAPERWORK

As general contractor and property manager, you will do best when all of your agreements are in writing. Verbal contracts are legal, but they usually end up unenforceable. Also, if there is a deviation from the original contract, you should insist on having a written change order executed.

When you pay your subcontractors for services rendered, make sure to have them sign a lien waiver preventing them from placing mechanic's and material man's liens against your property. This is crucial because, once a subcontractor has started work on your property, he has lien rights.

Unfortunately, too many property managers learn the value of well-documented agreements through bad experiences. You, on the other hand, have the opportunity to learn from the advice given in this chapter. If you follow good business principles in your dealings with subcontractors, you eliminate many risks.

CERTIFICATES OF INSURANCE

Before they do any work for you, obtain certificates of insurance from all of your independent contractors. Your insurance company may penalize you at the end of the year if you fail to keep a subcontractor's certificate of insurance on file. You could be charged additional money from the insurance company for allowing contractors who are not insured to do work on your building.

GETTING BIDS

It is good business sense to solicit bids from several subcontractors if the work that you need done is likely to be expensive. This can be an inconvenience, but it can also save you a lot of money. When you put your job out to bid, keep all of the bid packages identical. If the contractors do not bid on exactly the same work, the prices you get will be meaningless.

Additionally, beware of substitution clauses in the subcontractor's quote or estimate. If you specify a particular brand of an item, see to it that the contractor bids with that particular item. Frequently, contractors will put in an "or equal" clause in order to avoid providing specified materials. You should be suspicious when you see this clause in a quote. Substituting materials can end up making a huge difference when it comes to the cost of a job.

Be certain that the prices you are getting are based on the materials you want. Also, scrutinize the quote for omissions. Some sly contractors will purposely forget to include an aspect of the job to make their quote more attractive. When starting out as a property manager you can be an easy target for such unscrupulous behaviour.

LETTING CONTRACTORS INTO THE RENTAL UNITS

You should be careful if your contractors are going to be working in occupied rental units. Even if the contractors don't do anything wrong, tenants may make accusations.

To protect yourself, see that your subcontractors are bonded, and have the tenant present while the work is being done if that is possible. If the tenant can't be there, it may ease the situation if you promise to be there in their absence.

PREPARING FOR NIGHT CALLS

You may find that many of the top subcontractors do not necessarily have large businesses. They work alone, or with just a small crew, without fancy offices or full-time secretaries.

When you call during the day, you are likely to reach an answering machine. Since these subcontractors are in the field during the day and return calls at night, you will have trouble connecting with the best of them if you are unwilling to talk business after hours. It may be inconvenient to have to deal with night calls, but it can save you money. Because these small subcontractors have low overhead, their prices are often better than those of larger companies.

A SHORT CONCLUSION

Hopefully this chapter has opened your eyes to some of the realities of maintaining a rental property. Many novice landlords believe they can handle their routine maintenance with effortless ease. By now you should realize there is much more to maintenance and repairs than meets the eye.

As long as you take the necessary precautions and do your research in this area of business, you should do well. If you leap in with your eyes closed, you may learn to regret it.

Chapter 5:

Property Management & The Law

MUNICIPAL LEGISLATION

The category of law that affects property managers the most in the course of their functions is probably that of municipal legislation. The properties managed are consistently subject to:

- certain zoning and density regulations
- building standards/permits
- fire and safety regulations

Government security for the area is usually provided by a municipal police force and fire department, so it is important to acquire at least a broad understanding of the laws, by-laws, rules and regulations which govern the manager's actions on a local level.

Your most recurring contact with government is at this level; it is also the level at which you are most likely to find resolutions and answers. Explicit inquiries to the local city hall or municipal office can usually provide the needed answers very promptly and directly.

PROVINCIAL LEGISLATION

Provincial legislation is responsible for:
- Landlord and tenant matters, including
    ◦ rent review

- rent control legislation

- The administration of real estate assessment
- The various "Equipment and Labour" related laws which oversee and/or license the operation of:
    - elevators
    - boilers
    - unions (labour relations)
    - industrial safety
    - environmental concerns
    - public health issues
    - employment standards
    - operating engineers
    - condominiums

Although there is no practical limit to the laws and acts that could touch the property management, by far the most significant of all those mentioned are landlord tenant acts and rent review (control) acts.

This chapter will deal with the Ontario legislation. Although it may be considered typical on a Canada-wide basis, the legislation may be considerably different from province to province. Those practising outside of Ontario would be wise to also review the laws in their own jurisdictions.

The Ontario Act is known as "The Landlord and Tenant Act" and it has been amended many times in its history. It can be found online via www.ltb.gov.on.ca. Let's take a look at some of the most important clauses of "The Landlord and Tenant Act" in the section that follows.

THE LANDLORD AND TENANT ACT OF ONTARIO

There are five parts of The Landlord and Tenant Act of Ontario. The first three parts deal with landlord and tenant law in general, and provide some general definitions. Part IV concerns itself specifically with residential tenancies.

The first section of the act provides some specific definitions that are relevant in Part IV:

> 1 (b) "Landlord" includes Lessor, Owner, the person giving or permitting the occupation of the premises in question, and their

heirs and assigns and legal representatives; and in parts II and III also includes the person entitled to possession of the premises.

It would be safe to say that this definition includes the property manager.

1 (c) defines "Residential Premises" as:
(i) Any premises used or intended for use for residential purposes, and (ii) Land intended and used as a site for a mobile home used for residential purposes, whether or not the landlord also supplies the mobile home.

The definition then excludes:

(iii) premises occupied for business purposes with living accommodation attached under a single lease, unless the tenant occupying the living accommodation is a person other than the person occupying the premises for business purposes, in which case the living accommodation shall be deemed residential premises.

In 1 (e) a "tenant" is defined as including:

- lessee
- occupant
- sub-tenant
- under-tenant
- their assigns and legal representatives

SUMMARY OF PART IV OF THE ACT

The following sections refer specifically to the Ontario Landlord and Tenant Act. For province specific acts, please refer to the provincial and/or territorial government websites:

Alberta
www.servicealberta.gov.ab.ca/index.cfm?fuseaction=section:landlords

British Columbia
www.rto.gov.bc.ca

Manitoba
www.gov.mb.ca/finance/cca/rtb/coverpagertb.html

New Brunswick
www.gnb.ca/0062/Rentalsman/index-e.asp

Newfoundland and Labrador
www.gs.gov.nl.ca/cca/rt

Northwest Territories
www.justice.gov.nt.ca/RentalOffice/rentaloffice_legislation.shtml

Nova Scotia
www.gov.ns.ca/snsmr/consumer/resten

Nunavut
www.nunavuthousing.ca

Prince Edward Island
www.irac.pe.ca/rental

Quebec
www.rdl.gouv.qc.ca

Saskatchewan
www.justice.gov.sk.ca/Landlord-and-Tenant-Act

Yukon
www.housing.yk.ca

WHO IS AFFECTED?

The law gives both landlords and tenants specific rights and obligations, regardless of a written agreement. The landlord and tenant cannot waive these rights and obligations, despite any kind of written or verbal agreement.

Under an amendment, many dwellings occupied by roomers, boarders, and lodgers are also covered by Part IV of the Act.

WHAT IS A RESIDENTIAL DWELLING?

Part IV of the Act covers any property used (or intended for use) as a residence. This includes many different kinds of dwellings, such as:

- apartments
- houses
- townhouses
- mobile home sites

Some types of accommodations are not covered by the Act. We'll cover these further on in a section about dwellings not covered by the act.

TENANCY AGREEMENTS

A tenancy agreement is an arrangement between a landlord and a tenant that allows the tenant to live in a dwelling owned by the landlord. Once the agreement takes effect, the tenant is legally in possession of the dwelling, although the landlord is still technically the owner. A tenancy agreement may be in writing or it may be a verbal or implied agreement.

If the tenancy agreement is in writing:

> The landlord must deliver a copy of the agreement to the tenant within 21 days after the tenant has signed it. If the landlord does not meet the 21-day deadline, the tenant does not have to keep any of the promises set out in the tenancy agreement until a copy of it is delivered.

If the tenancy agreement is verbal:

Both the landlord and the tenant should have a clear understanding of the facilities and services included in the rent, as well as any other terms and conditions agreed upon, before the tenancy begins.

Although verbal agreements are valid, it is easier to prove the contents of a written agreement in the event of a dispute. Whether written or verbal, a tenancy agreement can be for a fixed term (whether a week, a month, a year or several years), or for an unspecified period of time, i.e. with no pre-set ending date.

SECURITY DEPOSITS

A landlord is allowed to ask a tenant to provide a security deposit at the beginning of a tenancy. By law, the amount of the security deposit is limited to the rent for one rental period (e.g. one week, month, etc.), up to a maximum of one month, even if the rental period is longer than one month.

A security deposit is to be used only for payment of rent for the last rental period of the tenancy. It cannot be used as payment for repair of damage to the dwelling, or for any other purpose. If a tenant believes the security deposit has been used for an unauthorized purpose, he can apply to District Court for a refund of the deposit plus interest.

As long as a landlord holds a security deposit, he must pay the tenant interest annually at the rate of 6% of the amount.

A landlord cannot require a tenant to provide post-dated cheques for the rent.

KEY MONEY

Ontario's Residential Rent Regulations Act makes it illegal to charge "key money" or any other payment in addition to a security deposit and the lawful rent for the dwelling. Neither a landlord nor a tenant can charge "key money" or any other payment from a tenant, a prospective tenant, or a sub-tenant in return for the opportunity to rent a residential dwelling.

Persons convicted of charging key money face a fine of up to $2,000 for individuals and up to $25,000 for corporations.

PRIVACY AND ACCESS

Tenants have the right to privacy in their rented dwellings. Occasionally, it may be necessary for a landlord to enter the dwelling. However, neither a landlord nor a landlord's representative has unlimited right of access.

To exercise the right to enter a dwelling, a landlord must:

- give the tenant 24 hours written notice
- specify in the notice the time the landlord plans to enter the dwelling
- enter the dwelling only during daylight hours

However, these requirements do not apply if:

- there is an emergency
- the tenancy agreement requires the landlord to regularly clean the dwelling (for example, in a rooming house)
- the tenancy agreement allows the landlord to show the dwelling to a prospective new tenant (during reasonable hours and only after notice of termination has been given)
- a tenant agrees, at the time of entry, to let the landlord enter the dwelling without 24 hours written notice

Neither the landlord nor the tenant can change the lock on any door giving entry to the dwelling without consent from the other.

REPAIRS AND MAINTENANCE

Landlords are responsible for keeping dwellings in good repair and fit for habitation, no matter what state a dwelling is in when the previous tenant moves out. Landlords must also comply with all health, safety and housing standards set by law.

If a dwelling is not properly maintained or repaired by a landlord, a tenant can apply to District Court. Among other things, the Court can:

- order the landlord to properly maintain the dwelling or make

any necessary repairs
- grant the tenant an "abatement of rent" (a temporary reduction in rent) because the landlord did not properly maintain or repair the dwelling

On the other hand, tenants are responsible for the ordinary cleanliness of the dwelling, except where the tenancy agreement makes it the landlord's responsibility to clean. Tenants must also repair any damage they or their guests wilfully or negligently cause to a dwelling.

If a tenant fails to pay the landlord for any damage to the dwelling caused by the tenant or any of the tenant's guests or to repair the damage, the landlord can apply to District Court to solve the problem.

Among other things, the Court can:

- order the tenant to pay the landlord for the damage
- order the tenant to clean or repair damage to the dwelling

Emergency Repairs

In emergencies, a tenant might pay to have crucial repairs done immediately. The tenant should be sure to keep detailed receipts for all repairs and submit them to the landlord for repayment.

A tenant would be smart to obtain the landlord's consent before subtracting the costs of such repairs from the rent. If the landlord does not accept the tenant's reason for the deduction, he may consider the tenant to be in arrears of rent, and take the dispute to District Court. If a tenant cannot convince the Court that the deduction was justified, the Court can order the tenant evicted.

SUBLETTING

A tenant (other than one in subsidized or public housing) is allowed to sublet, assign or otherwise part with possession of a dwelling in a rental building.

However, some tenancy agreements specify that the landlord has the right to consent to a subletting or assignment. This consent cannot be withheld by the landlord without reasonable cause.

By law, the landlord can charge the outgoing tenant reasonable expenses for giving such consent.

In the event of a dispute over subletting or assignment, a landlord or a tenant can apply to District Court.

MOBILE HOMES

Part IV of the Act also applies to landlords of mobile home parks and owners of mobile homes renting sites in these parks.

A tenant who owns a mobile home in such a park can sell or lease the home, even if it remains in the park. However, if the tenancy agreement allows the landlord to approve the sale or lease, the mobile home owner must get the landlord's consent before selling or leasing the home. A landlord cannot refuse consent without reasonable cause, and may not charge a fee except to cover reasonable expenses for giving this consent. Any dispute over a landlord's consent to a new tenant, and/or over expenses that can be charged by the landlord, can be referred to District Court.

A landlord cannot act as a tenant's agent in the sale or rental of a tenant's mobile home, unless the landlord and the tenant have a written contract to that effect. A landlord is permitted to charge only reasonable expenses for things such as entry, mobile home installation, exit and/or removal fees.

While a landlord is allowed to set reasonable standards for mobile home equipment, he or she cannot restrict the right of a tenant to purchase goods or services from the suppliers of his or her choice.

A landlord is obliged to provide garbage disposal and snow removal, and to maintain roads in a good state of repair, as well as plumbing, sewage, fuel and electrical systems in the park.

RENT INCREASES

Under the Residential Rent Regulation Act, the rent for most rental dwellings can be increased only once every twelve months. In addition, there are limits on the increase that can be charged.

A landlord must give a tenant proper written notice of a rent increase at least 90 days before the end of the tenancy period or term, regardless of the amount of increase.

ENDING A TENANCY

Under the Landlord and Tenant Act, a tenant is not obliged to move out of a rented dwelling simply because the term of the tenancy or lease has come to an end.

When a fixed-term tenancy agreement expires without the landlord and tenant entering into a new agreement, the tenancy is automatically renewed on a month-to-month basis under the same terms and conditions as the expired agreement.

A landlord or tenant who wants to terminate a weekly, monthly, yearly or any other tenancy must give proper written notice. If a landlord and a tenant mutually agree in writing to end a tenancy on a specific date, there is no need for a notice of termination to be given.

NOTICE OF TERMINATION

A notice of termination from either a landlord or a tenant must:

1) be in writing
2) identify the dwelling
3) specify the date the dwelling is to be vacated (the termination date)
4) be signed by the person giving the Notice (or by his/her agent)

A notice of termination from a landlord must also:

5) state the reason and supporting details for termination of a tenancy
6) point out that a tenant is not forced to leave simply because the notice has been served, but that the landlord may apply to Court to regain possession of the unit. A tenant has the right to dispute this application

Serving a Notice of Termination

A notice of termination from a tenant to a landlord (or to a landlord's agent) can be delivered personally or sent by regular mail. If the notice is sent by mail, the Landlord and Tenant Act assumes it is delivered on the third day after the date of mailing.

A Notice of Termination from the Tenant must be given to the Landlord as follows:

- For monthly tenancies, at least 60 days before the last day of the final month of the tenancy
- For fixed-term tenancies, at least 60 days before the last day of the tenancy
- For weekly tenancies, at least 28 days before the last day of the final week of the tenancy

Note: For monthly or weekly tenancies, the tenancy period does not necessarily mean "calendar" weeks or months. For instance, a monthly tenancy could begin March 15th. A tenant in this circumstance who wants to move in October must give a Notice of Termination no less than 60 days before October 14th (the last day of the final month of the tenancy). The termination then becomes effective on October 14th.

In the case of a notice of termination from a landlord to a tenant, the landlord must attempt to deliver the notice personally. However, if the tenant is away, or appears to be avoiding notification, the landlord can:

- hand the notice to a person in the tenant's dwelling if that person appears to be 18 years or older
- post the notice in a conspicuous place in the dwelling
- send the notice to the dwelling by registered mail (the Act assumes it is delivered on the third day after the date of mailing)

If a notice of termination from a tenant or a landlord is late – by even one day – it is not valid and must be given again. The same time limits as previously outlined again apply.

Termination by a Landlord

The Landlord and Tenant Act allows a landlord to end a tenancy only for certain reasons. The reason(s) for termination must be stated in detail in the landlord's Notice of Termination.

Early Termination by a Landlord

A landlord can terminate a tenancy before the end of the tenancy term (i.e. during the term of the agreement) for any of the following reasons:

- **failure to pay rent:** if a tenant fails to pay the rent on the day it is due
- **undue damage:** if a tenant or a tenant's guest wilfully or negligently cause damage to the dwelling
- **disturbing others:** if a tenant's conduct or the conduct of a tenant's guest cause a disturbance that substantially bothers any other tenant or the landlord
- **overcrowding:** if the number of people living in the dwelling is more than the number allowed by health, safety or housing standards
- **impairing safety:** if the safety of any other tenant is seriously impaired by a tenant's conduct
- **illegal acts:** if a tenant commits or permits an illegal act, or conducts an illegal business in the dwelling
- **misrepresenting income in public housing:** if a tenant in public or subsidized housing knowingly gives false information about his income or the income of other family members living in the dwelling

Procedures to Follow for Early Termination by a Landlord Due to:

1) failure to pay rent

   a) The landlord must give 20 days notice (in the case of a monthly, yearly or fixed-term tenancy).
   b) The tenant has 14 days (in case of a monthly, yearly or fixed-term tenancy) or 7 days (in the case of a daily or weekly tenancy) from receipt of notice to pay the rent owing.
   c) If the tenant does not pay the rent within the specified time period, and does not move out, the landlord can apply to District Court for an order permitting eviction of the tenant and/or ordering the tenant to pay the arrears in rent.

Note: It is illegal for a landlord to seize a tenant's personal property if the tenant is behind in rent.

2) damage
3) disturbances
4) impairing safety
5) overcrowding

In any of these instances, the following procedures apply:

- The landlord must give 20 days notice.
- The tenant has 7 days to correct the situation.
- If the tenant fails to correct the situation within 7 days, the landlord can apply for a court order to evict the tenant.

Note: if the tenant corrects the breach within the allotted 7 days, the notice of termination becomes invalid. However, if, within six months, there is a second breach by the tenant of any of the items 2-5 above, the landlord can give only 14 days notice and can immediately apply for a court order permitting the tenant's eviction.

6) illegal acts
7) misrepresentation of income in public housing
In these last two instances, the following procedures apply: The landlord must give 20 days notice and can apply immediately for a court order permitting the tenant's eviction.

Reasons for Termination by a Landlord at the End of a Tenancy

A landlord can terminate a tenancy at the end of the tenancy term for any of the reasons noted above under early termination, and for the following additional reasons:

- the landlord's own use
  - if the landlord needs the dwelling for accommodation for himself; for his spouse; for children of the landlord or spouse; or for the parents of the landlord or spouse

- persistent late rent
    - if a tenant has persistently failed in the past to pay the rent on the day it is due

- ceases to qualify
    - if a tenant no longer qualifies for tenancy in public or subsidized housing

- employment ended
    - if a tenant was provided the dwelling by an employer and the tenant's employment ends

- demolition, conversion, major repairs, or renovation, or failed agreement
    - If a tenant must move because:
        - The landlord plans to demolish the building.
        - The landlord plans to put the rental property to some other use (i.e. as an office) and will no longer rent it as a dwelling.
        - The landlord plans extensive repairs or renovations that require a building permit and vacant possession is required. This is because it would be impractical or unsafe for a tenant to continue living in the dwelling while the work is underway.
        - The tenancy is the result of an agreement to purchase a proposed condominium unit, and the agreement falls through.

Procedures to Follow for the Termination by a Landlord at the End of a Tenancy:

- landlord's own use:
    - The landlord must give 60 days notice before the end of a tenancy.
    - If the tenant does not move from the dwelling by the termination date, the landlord can apply for a court order allowing eviction of the tenant.

- persistent late rent
- ceasing to qualify
- termination of caretaker's tenancy
    - Special provisions apply to a landlord's termination of the tenancy of a caretaker, janitor, watchman, security guard, or superintendent.
    - Unless otherwise agreed, the tenancy ends on the day the employment ends; the person has one week, rent-free, in which to move out of the dwelling.
- failed condominium sale

In any of these instances:

- The landlord must give 60 days notice (in the case of a monthly, yearly, or fixed-term tenancy) or 28 days notice (in the case of a weekly tenancy) before the end of the tenancy.
- If the tenant does not move by the termination date, the landlord can apply for a court order.

Demolition, Conversion, Major Repairs or Renovation

Under the Rental Housing Protection Act, certain restrictions apply to activities that reduce the existing supply of affordable rental housing in Ontario. Municipal approval may be necessary to convert, renovate, extensively repair, sever or change the use of rental housing. Where the Act applies, such approval must be obtained before a landlord can serve a Notice of Termination. A copy of the approval must be attached to the Notice of Termination.

Failure to obtain approval where necessary, and/or failure to provide a tenant with a copy of the approval along with a Notice of Termination is illegal.

In order to terminate such tenancy:

- the landlord must give 120 days notice before the end of tenancy
- a tenant who receives a notice for any of these reasons may leave

- before the 120 days by giving the landlord at least 10 days written notice that he will vacate the dwelling on this earlier, specified date
- a tenant who receives a notice because extensive repairs or renovations will be done has the right, if he so advises the landlord in writing before leaving, to re-occupy the dwelling once the work is completed
- if the tenant wants to re-occupy the unit, he is entitled to the lowest rent that would be charged to any other tenant
- a tenant who wants to exercise this "right of first refusal" must give or send the landlord, by registered mail, a forwarding address where he can be reached while the work is being done

Note: A landlord who wants to terminate at the end of a tenancy must make the termination effective on the last day of the fixed term or period of the tenancy. A weekly or monthly tenancy period does not necessarily mean "calendar" weeks or months. For instance, a monthly tenancy could begin March 15th. A landlord who wants a tenant to move in October would have to make the termination effective October 14th and follow the time limits for serving a Notice of Termination.

Disputing a Termination by a Landlord

A tenant is entitled to dispute a landlord's reason for ending a tenancy. If a tenant intends to dispute a termination, he is not required to move out of the rental dwelling unless the District Court subsequently orders the tenant to be evicted.

A TENANT'S RIGHTS AND LEGAL REMEDIES

A tenant has the right to apply to District Court:

- for an order requiring the landlord to make repairs
- for authorization of repairs which have already been done by a tenant
- for an "abatement of rent" (a temporary reduction of rent) if the dwelling has not been properly maintained or repaired
- to end a tenancy

- for return of a security deposit and/or for payment of interest on the deposit

A LANDLORD'S RIGHTS AND LEGAL REMEDIES

A landlord has the right to apply to District Court:

- for an order declaring a tenancy ended
- for a 'writ of possession' (eviction order)
- for payment of arrears of rent or compensation for damage
- to enforce a tenant's notice of termination (or written agreement to terminate)

EVICTIONS

A landlord can regain possession of a rental dwelling if a tenant has moved out or abandoned the dwelling. However, if the tenant has not moved, the landlord must obtain a court order and a writ of possession before the tenant can be removed. A tenant can be physically removed only by a sheriff acting on a court order.

VITAL SERVICES

A landlord cannot withhold the reasonable supply of vital services that are required to be provided under a tenancy agreement. Vital services include:

- heat
- fuel
- electricity
- gas
- water

In addition, a landlord cannot interfere with these vital services, whether or not the landlord is obliged to provide them under the tenancy agreement.

TENANT SECURITY

The District Court must refuse a landlord an order permitting eviction if the Court decides that the landlord:

- has not lived up to his obligations
- wants to evict a tenant because he complained about the landlord's violation of health, safety, or housing laws
- is retaliating against a tenant who sought to exercise his legal rights
- wants to evict a tenant because he belongs to a tenant's association or is trying to organize one
- wants to evict a tenant because of the presence of children (except in cases of overcrowding or where the dwelling is unsuitable for children)

In addition, the Court may refuse an eviction order where it would be unfair to not do so.

POSTING THE ACT

A landlord of a residential rental building with more than one unit and common facilities (such as a lobby) must post and keep posted a copy of Act IV of the Landlord and Tenant Act (or the official summary) in a place where it can be easily seen.

The legal name of the landlord, and an address at which the landlord can be served with notices, must also be posted.

OFFENCES AND PENALTIES

The Landlord and Tenant Act allows for fines up to $2,000 for offences under the Act, including:

- altering locks
- withholding or interfering with vital services
- failing to post a copy of Part IV of the Act (or the official summary), and/or the landlord's legal name and address
- evicting without a court order

- seizing a tenant's property for non-payment of rent

DWELLINGS NOT COVERED BY THE ACT

Some types of accommodation are not covered by the Landlord and Tenant Act. Exemptions include:

- dwellings occupied for business or agricultural purposes with accommodation attached, where there is a single lease and the same person occupies both dwellings
- dwellings in which the occupant shares bathroom or kitchen facilities with the owner and/or members of the owner's immediate family living in the same building
- dwellings occupied by members of a non-profit co-operative housing corporation
- accommodation for the traveling and vacationing public in hotels, motels, resorts, cottages, trailer parks, etc.
- accommodation in hospital, nursing homes, etc.
- accommodation for penal or correctional purposes
- short-term accommodation provided as an emergency shelter
- accommodation related to employment on a farm
- accommodations rented as vacation homes for seasonal or temporary periods not longer than four months

In addition, Part IV of the Act does not cover certain types of accommodations provided by educational institutions to students and staff. Part IV will not apply if:

- most of the residents are under 18 years of age
- all major questions related to the accommodation are decided after consultation with a residents' council or association

However, if the accommodation has its own self-contained bathroom and kitchen facilities, and is intended for year-round accommodation by full-time students or staff, it is covered by Part IV.

Conclusion

As property management can be done by the most novice individuals, it is a task that one needs to determine they'd like to pursue. It can be a cumbersome task for someone that does not fully understand everything that is involved. You've read about the various types of property management, working with and screening for tenants, reviewed the various aspects of leases in detail, reviewed aspects of a property as it relates to repairs and maintenance, and finally read about laws affecting property managers.

Remember to use this publication as a resource when managing your various properties. With the wealth of information contained within the previous pages, it will be hard to remember everything. A quick glance through the table of contents will direct you to the section that will apply to your situation.

It has been the goal of this publication to enlighten those new to property management on the various aspects that fall under its umbrella. In addition, for those with some experience in property management, this book should have taken you to the next level in your various dealings, perhaps giving you some ideas on how you can leverage your time and efforts more effectively.

Good luck and happy investing!

Glossary

ABANDONMENT: A relinquishment or surrender of property or rights. Abandonment of leased premises refers to the relinquishing of the premises by the tenant without consent of the owner before the lease expires.

ABATEMENT: In real estate, a reduction of rent, interest, or an amount due.

ABSTRACT OF TITLE: A summary of all deeds, wills, and legal proceedings which show the nature of a person's right to a given estate, together with the mortgages, judgments, etc. which constitute liens or encumbrances thereon.

ACCEPTANCE: The act of taking or receiving something that is offered.

ACCOUNT: A detailed statement of receipts and payments of money or of trade transactions that have taken place between two or more persons.

ACCOUNTING: The theory and system of setting up and maintaining the book of a business organization; analyzing the operation of a business from a study of income and expenses.

ACCREDITED MANAGEMENT ORGANIZATION (AMO): A designation conferred by the Institute of Real Estate Management of the National Association of Realtors to real estate management firms which are under the direction of a Certified Property Manager (CPM) and which comply with stipulated requirements as to accounting procedure, performance, and protection of funds entrusted to them.

AD VALOREM: Tax that is levied against property, based on its value.

ADJUSTMENT: In the law of insurance, it is the settlement of the amount to be received by the insured.

ADVERSE POSSESSION: The actual, visible, hostile, notorious, exclusive, and continuous possession of another's land under a claim of title; possession for a statutory period may be a means of acquiring title.

AFFIDAVIT OF SERVICE: A sworn statement that an eviction notice has been served properly.

AGENCY MANAGEMENT: Management by an agency, authorized to do so, or property owned by another.

AGENT: A person who enters into a legal, fiduciary, and confidential arrangement with a second party and is authorized to act for that party.

AGGREGATE RENT: The total or gross rent amount for a lease term.

ALLODIAL SYSTEM: Form of private landholding in which land is held in absolute ownership.

ALTERATION: The process of changing the function of a property.

AMORTIZATION: Of assets, a means of gradually reducing the book value of a fixed asset by spreading its depreciation over a period of time; of debt, a means of gradually retiring an obligation by making regular payments of principal and interest over a period of time.

ANCHOR TENANT: A key tenant in a shopping centre that will attract other businesses as well as customers.

ANNUAL STATEMENT: In real estate, a fully detailed and annotated statement of all income and expense items involving cash and covering a twelve-consecutive-month period of operation of an individual property; and including the disposition and application of net funds for the period concerned and accumulated funds from prior periods. Variations in form and content are effected to conform to owner directives.

APARTMENT: A residential unit found in a variety of properties such as walk-ups, garden-type projects, elevator buildings, and condominiums.

APARTMENT BUILDING: A building designed for the separate housing of two or more families and where mutual services are supplied for comfortable and convenient occupancy.

APPRAISAL: An estimate of value is the process through which conclusions of property value are obtained; it also refers to the report setting for the estimate and conclusion of value.

ASSESSMENT: Amount charged against each owner or tenant of a property to fund its operation.

ASSET: Any physical property or right that is owned and has a monetary value, generally appearing as one of the major categories on the financial balance sheet.

ASSET MANAGEMENT: A sophisticated form of property management under which the managing agent organizes, operates, and assumes the risk of the total real estate business venture and whose concern extends beyond net operating income.

AUTOMATIC RENEWAL CLAUSE: A lease provision that automatically ensures renewal of the lease unless either the tenant or the landlord notifies the other party of a desire to terminate the agreement.

BASE RENT: The minimum amount of rent payable under the terms of a percentage lease.

BASE-UNIT-APPROACH: A method of establishing rental rates in which a typical unit within a specific submarket is defined and becomes the standard against which all similar units may be measured.

BOARD OF DIRECTORS: The official governing body of a corporation, including condominiums and co-operatives.

BROKER: An agent who buys or sells for a principal on a commission without having title to the property.

BUDGET: A prediction of income and expenses over a specific time period for a particular property.

BUILDING CODES: Ordinances specifying minimum standards of construction of buildings for the protection of public safety and health.

BULK USER: A commercial enterprise that utilizes a large quantity of office space.

BYLAWS: Regulations that provide specific procedures for handling routine matters in a condominium operation.

CAPITAL: Any form of wealth capable of being used to create more wealth.

CAPITALIZATION: The process of converting a property's anticipated future income into value.

CASH FLOW: The amount of cash available after all payments have been made for operating expenses and mortgage principal and interest.

CASHIER: The person in the property management firm who records all income, bills accounts, and draws buildings' payrolls.

CEDE: To assign or transfer.

CERTIFIED PROPERTY MANAGER (CPM): The professional designation conferred by the Real Estate Institute of Canada on individuals who distinguish themselves in the areas of education, experience, and ethics.

CHATTEL: A movable article of property other than land, buildings, or things legally and physically annexed or attached to real property.

CLASSIFIED ADVERTISEMENT: A basic medium for briefly announcing space for rent, which usually appears in a special section of a newspaper.

CMHC: Canada Mortgage and Housing Corporation, a Crown Corporation that administers the National Housing Act.

COMMERCIAL PROPERTY: Real property used for the conduct of retail or service businesses and inviting public patronage by display of signs, merchandise, advertising, and other stimulants for public participation.

COMMON AREA: Space that is not used and occupied exclusively by tenants, such as lobbies, corridors, and stairways; in a condominium, the property in which a unit owner has an undivided interest.

COMMON AREA MAINTENANCE CLAUSE: A provision in I.C. & I. (Invoice Costs and Charges) Leases which states that the tenant must pay a share of the cost of operating and maintaining the centre and the manner in which these charges will be assessed.

COMMON EXPENSES: The costs of operating, managing, maintaining, and repairing a condominium's common areas and administering the condominium association.

COMMON LAW: A system of laws, originating in England and based on court decisions, which treats everyone equally, regardless of geographic or social status.

COMPLEX: A group of buildings that together form a single comprehensive group.

CONCESSIONS: Things conceded or granted in real estate, to induce the making of a lease and sale.

CONDEMNATION: The taking of private property for public use; also the official act to terminate the use of real property for nonconformance with governmental regulations or due to the existence of hazards to public health and safety.

CONDOMINIUM: A form of ownership that combines absolute ownership of an apartment-like unit and joint ownership of areas used in common with others.

CONDOMINIUM ASSOCIATION: A condominium's governing body to which every unit owner automatically belongs.

CONDOMINIUM UNIT: A three-dimensional space of air located within the walls, floor, and ceiling of the condominium structure.

CONDUIT: An ownership vehicle that passes income tax benefits or liabilities directly through to individual investors.

CONSULTATION: A service offered to owners whose properties do not require ongoing management but who do need advice on specific problems, such as rehabilitation, modernization, or property conversions.

CONSUMER PRICE INDEX: A figure constructed monthly by Statistics Canada that weighs products by their importance and compares prices to those of a selected base year, expressing current prices as a percentage of prices in the base year.

CONTRACT: An agreement entered into by two or more legally competent parties by the terms of which one or more of the parties, for a consideration, undertakes to do or refrain from doing some legal act or acts.

CONTROLLABLE EXPENSE: An operating expense over which management has definite responsibility and control.

COOPERATIVE: A corporation that owns real estate, usually a multi-family dwelling, including the building and land on which it is built; individual shareholders do not own their units but have the right to live in them.

CORPORATION: A form of business organization created by statute law, which is legally considered a separate entity.

CORRECTIVE MAINTENANCE: Ongoing repairs that must be made to a building and its equipment.

CREDIT INVESTIGATING AGENCY: A firm that gathers and records any information that has a bearing on a consumer's credit capacity and reports to its clients on a fee per report basis.

CUSTODIAL MAINTENANCE: The policing and housekeeping duties associated with a property.

DATE OF COMMENCEMENT: In a lease on real property, the date upon which the lease term starts and rental begins to accrue; the day upon which the tenant comes into possession subject to the provisions of the lease.

DATE OF LEASE: The date that the lease instrument is signed by the contracting parties.

DATE OF TERMINATION: In a lease on real property, the date upon which the lease term ends, rentals cease to accrue, and the tenant gives up possession to the owner or agent.

DEED: An instrument in writing, duly executed and delivered, that conveys title or an interest in real property.

DEFERRED MAINTENANCE: Ordinary maintenance that is not performed and negatively affects a property's use and value.

DEFICIENCY DISCOUNT: A reduction in rent to induce a tenant to accept a substandard apartment.

DEMISED PREMISES: Property covered by a lease agreement.

DEPRECIATION: Any decline in the value of a physical asset, usually resulting from physical deterioration (ordinary wear and tear), functional depreciation, and economic obsolescence; the process of gradually converting a fixed asset into an expense.

DIRECT HOUSING SUBSIDY: A financial grant that increases the housing supply available to specified households (i.e. low and moderate income, handicapped, elderly).

DIRECT-MAIL ADVERTISING: A medium of promotion through letters, cards, or brochures, sent by mail to potential customers and which relies heavily on specialized mailing lists.

DIRECTOR OF PROPERTY MANAGEMENT: The person in a property management organization who oversees the activities of the firm's property supervisors.

DIRECT SOLICITATION: A procedure in which a property manager specifically asks an owner for the management of a building.

DISABILITY CLAUSE: A special lease covenant that provides for the alteration of the lease terms or the termination of the lease before expiration, in the event that the tenant is physically disabled and unable to continue use of the leased premises. Most often included in leases for residential property.

DISPLAY ADVERTISEMENT: A large paid notice designed to attract the public's attention in marketing a new property, especially commercial and industrial space.

DUPLEX: One building with two separate living units.

DWELLING UNIT: A place to live in, residence, abode.

EASEMENT: A right or interest in land of another that entitles the holder thereof to some use, privilege, or benefit out of or over said land.

ECONOMIC LIFE: The period of time for which a building can be used to produce assets or services.

ECONOMIC OVERSUPPLY: Vacancy that occurs entirely because of consumer inability to pay current rents.

ECONOMIC RENT RAISE: An increase in rent determined by market shortage and general consumer income level.

ECONOMIC SHORTAGE: A condition, based on a technical shortage, occurring when there are more able-to-buy consumers than available rental units.

ELECTRONIC DATA PROCESSING (EDP) BOOKKEEPING SYSTEM: A computerized bookkeeping system that issues accurate records and establishes controls over income and expenses.

ENCUMBRANCE: An outstanding claim or lien recorded against a property or any legal right to the use of the property by another person who is not the owner.

EQUALIZATION: The raising or lowering of assessed values for tax purposes in a particular county or taxing district to make them equal to assessments in other counties or districts.

ESCALATION CLAUSE: A provision in a lease that guarantees automatic rent adjustments for increased operating expenses.

ESTABLISHED NEIGHBOURHOOD: A sound, healthy area in which all the land has been developed and families and social institutions are stable.

EVICTION: The legal ejection of tenants and their possessions from the leased premises by the landlord.

EVICTION NOTICE: A written notice to a tenant to vacate the leased premises within a specified time for infractions of the lease or other specified causes.

EXCLUSIVE RIGHT: In leases, this reserves the right for one tenant exclusively to conduct a certain business in the leased property during the term of the lease.

EXECUTIVE PROPERTY MANAGER: The person who is directly responsible for all management policies, procedures, and employees in a property management firm.

FACILITY: A building, special room, etc., that facilitates or makes possible some activity, e.g. a recreation facility.

FEE SIMPLE OWNERSHIP: The greatest and most absolute ownership of land, subject to the least number of restrictions.

FEUDALISM: A political and economic system of the ninth to fifteenth centuries in which the king had supreme right over the land, which then was divided among lords and their vassals based on conditions of homage and service.

FINANCIAL ANALYSIS: A complete evaluation of real estate as an investment including valuation, depreciation, tax benefits, and cash flow calculations.

FISCAL SERVICES: Duties other than the management of real property that are assumed by management firms to assist corporations.

FIXED ASSETS: Properties, goods, or other things of value that cannot be readily sold or otherwise converted on short notice, at their true or fair value. Things possessed mainly of value if used as is, and of little value if removed, such as trade fixtures and machinery.

FIXED EXPENSES: Expenses that do not vary with occupancy (e.g. fire insurance) and that have to be paid whether the property is occupied or vacant. Fixed expenses are not necessarily or absolutely fixed in amount, and tend to vary from year to year.

FIXTURE: An article of personal property attached permanently to a building or to land so that it becomes part of the real estate.

FLAT BUILDING: Two or more separate suites of living quarters, one above the other or contiguous to each other, each having independent means of ingress and egress and otherwise independent of each other.

FOUR-PLEX: A flat building of four separate living units.

FURNISHINGS: Fittings, appliances, and other chattels used in a house or a room.

GARDEN APARTMENT: A low-rise building designated for multi-family living, usually located in a suburban area; also, an apartment in the basement or on the ground floor having access to a garden or lawn.

GRADUATED RENT: Rent which has two or more levels in the same lease term.

GROSS FLOOR AREA: The total floor area (including the common area) or space that is not used exclusively by tenants.

GROSS LEASE: An agreement in which the tenant pays a fixed rental and the owner pays all the expenses associated with operating the property.

GROUND LEASE: A lease for land only on which the tenant usually owns the building or is required to build his own building as specified by the lease. Such leases are usually long-term net leases; tenants' rights and obligations continue until the lease expires or is terminated for default.

HEATING, VENTILATING, AND AIR-CONDITIONING (HVAC) SYSTEM: The unit regulating the even distribution of heat and fresh air throughout a building.

HIGHEST AND BEST USE: The most productive use to which real property may be put for the most desirable period of time considering all economic factors.

"HOLD HARMLESS" CLAUSE: One party in a lease agrees not to hold another liable for certain acts, or certain unforeseen circumstances, as specified in the lease.

HOLDOVER TENANT: A tenancy whereby the tenant retains possession of leased premises after his lease has expired, and the landlord by continuing to accept rent from the tenant thereby agrees to tenant's continued occupancy as defined by provincial laws.

HOME: A house, apartment, or other shelter that is the fixed residence of an individual, a family or a household.

HOTEL APARTMENT: An apartment building offering hotel services to residential tenants, usually on a permanent basis.

HOUSING UNIT: Any residential arrangement that constitutes separate living quarters.

INDEX ESCALATION CLAUSE: A provision ensuring rent adjustments in an amount equal to the annual change in a specified index, usually the Consumer Price Index.

INDIRECT INFLUENCE: An impact on housing as a result of monetary, fiscal and credit policies.

INDIVIDUAL METER: A utility-measuring device for each tenant in a multi-unit building.

INFLATION: An economic condition occurring when the money supply increases in relation to goods. It is associated with rising wages, costs, and decreasing purchasing power.

IN-HOUSE MANAGEMENT: Management originating from within an organization or company, i.e. by the staff of the corporation owning the property, rather than brought in from outside.

INSTITUTIONAL ADVERTISING: A technique designed to raise the prestige of the property management firm or building through some promotional medium, such as billboards or wall displays.

JOB DESCRIPTION: A written outline of the specific duties and requirements for each position in a company.

JOINT TENANTS: Two or more owners of a parcel of land who have been specifically named in one conveyance as joint tenants. Upon the death of a joint tenant, his interest passes to the surviving joint tenant(s) by the right of survivorship, which is the important element of joint tenancy.

LAISSEZ-FAIRE: An economic philosophy stating that government should not interfere with commerce and economic affairs.

LANDLORD: One who owns property and leases it to a tenant.

LEASE: A contract given by the landlord to the tenant for use of possession of real property, for a specified time, and in exchange for fixed payments.

LEASEHOLD: Land held under a lease.

LEASING AGENT: The person in a management firm directly responsible for renting space in assigned properties.

LESSEE: The tenant in a lease.

LESSOR: The landlord in a lease.

LEVERAGE: The use of borrowed funds so that the investor realizes a profit not only on his/her own cash investment but also on the lender's money.

LEVY: To impose or assess a tax on a property or activity.

LIFE-SUPPORT SYSTEMS: The safety and security procedures that are adopted by a property's management.

LIMITED PARTNERSHIP: A business arrangement that allows certain partners to invest, take no part in the management, and assume limited liability.

LISTING CLERK: The person in a property management firm who distributes leads to rental agents.

LOCATION: A reference to the comparative advantages of one site in consideration of factors such as transportation, convenience, and social benefits.

LOFT BUILDING: A structure of two or more stories originally designed for industrial use.

LOW-RISE: An apartment building containing five stories or less.

MAINTENANCE: Care, preservation; keeping in good physical and operating condition and appearance.

MANAGEMENT AGREEMENT: A written contract in which a property owner contracts the management of a property to an individual manager or firm and which details all rights and obligations of both parties.

MANAGEMENT FEE: Monetary consideration paid monthly or otherwise for the performance of management duties.

MANAGEMENT PLAN: An outline of a property's physical and fiscal management that is directed toward achieving the owner's goals.

MA-PA MANAGEMENT: The management of real property by a husband and wife team where typically the wife assumes the duties of renting and record keeping and the husband performs the maintenance chores.

MARKET ANALYSIS: The process of placing a property in a specific space market and then evaluating it by those market standards.

MARKET APPROACH: A method of estimating a property's value by comparing it with similar properties that have been sold recently.

MARKET VALUE: The highest price that a buyer, who is ready, willing, and able, but not compelled to buy, would pay, and the lowest a seller, who is ready, willing and able but not compelled to sell, would accept.

MARKET SURVEY: The process of gathering information about specific comparable properties and comparing it to data concerning the subject property in order to weigh its advantages and disadvantages.

MECHANIZED BOOKKEEPING SYSTEM: An accounting system that relies on a bookkeeping machine to post accounts and uses one trust fund account with a subsidiary ledger for each property.

MERCHANDISING: An aspect of marketing that creates a desire for a particular article that people use almost universally by pointing out features in the item that will appeal to the buyer.

MID-RISE APARTMENT: A multi-family structure that ranges from six to nine stories and is found in both cities and suburbs.

MODERNIZATION: The process of replacing original equipment with similar features of up-to-date design.

MONTH-TO-MONTH TENANCY: An agreement to rent or lease for consecutive and continuing monthly periods until terminated by proper prior notice either by the landlord or the tenant. Notice of termination must precede the commencement date of the final month of occupancy. The time period of prior notice is usually established by provincial law.

MORTGAGE: A conditional pledge of property to a creditor as security against a debt.

NATIONAL HOUSING ACT: The National Housing Act (1954), revising and superseding previous housing and mortgage policies; it provides for insuring NHA loans made by approved lenders and for direct mortgage lending under a variety of programmes by Canada Mortgage and Housing Corporation (CMHC).

NEIGHBOURHOOD ANALYSIS: A study of a neighbourhood and comparison of it with the broader economic and geographic area of which it is a part, to determine why individuals and businesses are attracted to it.

NET (SINGLE-NET) LEASE: An agreement in which the tenant pays the rent and also certain expenses connected with the leased premises.

NET-NET LEASE: An agreement in which the tenant pays all maintenance and operating expenses plus property taxes.

NET-NET-NET (TRIPLE-NET) LEASE: An agreement in which the tenant pays maintenance and operating expenses, property taxes, and insurance.

NET OPERATING INCOME BEFORE DEPRECIATION: The income remaining after operating expenses have been deducted from the effective gross income.

NONCONTROLLABLE EXPENSES: Items such as real estate taxes, insurance, and labour union wages over which the property management has no control.

NOTICE TO VACATE: A legal notice requiring tenants to remove their possessions from the premises within a stated period of time or upon a specified day and date, and to deliver up the premises to the owner, agent or designated successor.

NUISANCE RENT RAISE: The rent raise a tenant will pay to avoid the expense, discomfort, and inconvenience of moving.

OCCUPANCY AGREEMENT: A residential lease.

OFFICE BUILDING: A single-story or multi-story structure, usually divided into individual offices, where business is carried out or services provided and space is offered for rent or lease.

OFFICE LANDSCAPING: A technique in space planning that utilizes floor space in an open manner.

OFF-SITE MANAGEMENT: Management of a property by persons not residing or keeping office hours at the subject property.

OPERATING EXPENSES: Generally denotes all expenses necessary to maintain the production of income from operation of a property; the difference between Effective Gross Income and Net Operating Income (NOI).

OPTION: A right given for a valuable consideration to purchase or lease property at a future date for a specified price and terms; the right may or may not be exercised at the option holder's (optionee's) discretion.

OWNERSHIP: Legal right of possession; proprietorship.

PARCEL: A separable, separate, or distinct part, portion or section of land often identified as a numbered lot, with designated boundaries.

PARTITION SUIT: A legal action to dissolve a tenancy in common by requiring one of the common owners to purchase the interest of another owner or to sell an interest to another common owner or to liquidate or sell the entire fee estate, all based upon a stipulated and established fair market price; prorating the proceeds in event of a sale of the fee to others in proportion to the respective legal interests of the common owners and after deducting all legal costs as determined by the court.

PERCENTAGE-OF-GROSS FEE: A property manager's regular compensation based on a given percentage of monthly gross collections.

PERCENTAGE RENT: Rent that is based on a percentage of the gross sales or net income of the tenant, often against a guaranteed minimum.

PERSONALITY: Personal property.

PHYSICAL LIFE: The length of time for which a building is a sound structure, which depends on the quality of maintenance.

PLOT: A scale drawing of a parcel of land or several parcels of land, oriented as to directions, and important facilities, and showing the location of buildings, right-of-way, easements, etc.; a piece of land.

POLICY: Management guideline within which decisions are to be made.

POTENTIAL GROSS INCOME: The income that a property will produce with 100% occupancy. The potential gross income is generally derived by multiplying the rental value per unit times the number of units in the building.

PREVENTATIVE MAINTENANCE: A program of regular inspection and care that allows potential problems to be prevented or at least detected and solved before major repairs are needed.

PRINCIPAL: In property management, the property owner who authorizes an agent to act for him.

PRINCIPLE OF DIMINISHING RETURNS: A valuation principle which states that when successive increments of one or more factors of production are added to fixed amounts of the other factors there is a resulting enhancement of income (in dollars, benefits, or amenities), initially at an increasing rate to a point of maximum return and then decreasing until eventually the increment to value becomes increasingly less than the value of the added factor or factors. The Principle of Diminishing Returns is sometimes referred to as the Principle of Variable Proportions.

PROPERTY ANALYSIS: A complete description of a piece of real estate, including its accommodation, architectural design, and physical condition.

PROPERTY MANAGEMENT: A service profession in which someone other than the owner supervises a property's operation, according to the owner's objectives.

PROPERTY MANAGER: A professional who administers real estate according to the owner's objectives.

PROPERTY SUPERVISOR: The person who has direct responsibility for specific properties, including tenant, owner and personnel contact.

PROPRIETARY LEASE: A document that gives a shareholder in a cooperative the right to occupy a unit under certain conditions.

PROSPECT: A potential customer.

PUBLIC AREA: A space in a property for general use and not restricted for use by any lease or other agreements, such as a lobby, corridor, or court.

PUBLIC HOUSING PROGRAM: The principal form of federal housing assistance for low-income families.

PURCHASING AGENT: The person in the management firm who supervises the purchase of goods and services.

QUALIFICATION: The process of judging a prospective tenant's acceptability.

REAL ESTATE: The land and any improvements found on it; the term is often applied to non-agricultural property, which accommodates individuals, business, and industry.

REAL ESTATE CYCLE: A period of time in the real estate industry that experiences regular and recurring economic changes.

REAL ESTATE INSTITUTE OF CANADA (REIC): A professional association for persons who meet standards of experience, education, and ethics with the objective of continually improving their respective managerial skills by mutual education and exchange of ideas and experiences. The Institute represents the specialized area of property management, real estate brokerage and marketing, leasehold acquisition, real estate finance and land planning and development, and administers the designations CPM, ALO, CMR, CRF, CLP, and FRI.

REAL ESTATE SECURITY: A form of personal property (stocks and bonds) secured by real property and which is evidence of real estate ownership or indebtedness.

REGIONAL ANALYSIS: Identification of the general economic and demographic conditions and physical aspects of the area surrounding a property and determining which trends affect it.

REHABILITATION: The process of lengthening a building's economic life within its present design by restoring it to a well-maintained condition.

REMINDER NOTICE: A notice sent to tenant when rent is delinquent.

RENT: Periodic payment made for the use of a property over a period of time.

RENTAL INQUIRY CARD: A record of all prospects that have called or have visited a property, used for future reference when other units become available.

RENTAL LEDGER: A written record noting tenants' names, units, phone numbers, rents, security deposits, and other leasing information.

RENTAL PRICE LEVEL: An indicator that moves up and down in response to supply and demand and reveals the economic strength of the real estate market.

RENTAL SCHEDULE: A listing of rental rates for units or space in a given building.

RENT BILL: An invoice sent to tenants just before the rent is due.

RENT CONTROL: Government regulations imposed on residential properties for the purpose of limiting the increase in rents.

RENT RECEIPT: A record of payment received.

RENT ROLL: A balance sheet for the account of each rental area, listing tenants' names and their unit numbers, along with all income payable and paid.

RESIDENT MANAGER: The person who usually lives in the property and is responsible for general administration and maintenance of the property as well as supervising its personnel and resources.

RETAIL PROPERTIES: Establishments in which goods and services are sold directly to individuals and households.

RETROFITTING: The replacement of some fixtures or facilities in a building with more energy-efficient fittings.

RIDER: An amendment to a lease, signed by both the lessor and the lessee.

RIGHT OF RE-ENTRY: The act of resuming possession of lands, or tenements, in pursuance of a right reserved by the owner on parting with the possession. Leases usually contain a clause providing that the owner may terminate the lease, and re-enter for non-payments of rent or breach of any of the covenants by the tenant.

RULES AND REGULATIONS: Guidelines for personal behaviour in any property; measures that affect relations among neighbours also may be included.

SALE: The transfer from one person to another for a consideration of the possession and right of use of some particular article of value to both parties.

SECURITY DEPOSIT: Money advanced by a tenant and held by an owner or manager for a specific period of time to cover possible damages and ensure faithful performance of the lease by the tenant.

SERVICE REQUEST CLERK: Member of the property management firm who arranges for all maintenance requests to be handled.

SLUM: A core area of a city in which overcrowding and deterioration are evident.

SLUM CLEARANCE: The process of razing urban real estate when it has deteriorated to a point at which salvage is impossible.

SOCIAL OBSOLESCENCE: A loss in value brought about by social conditions; i.e. a condition occurring in neighbourhoods with desirable locations but in which homes are too large for present-day families.

SOLE PROPRIETORSHIP: A form of business organization in which an individual owns and manages the entire enterprise.

SPACE: In real estate, an area providing for residential, commercial, or industrial occupancy.

STANDARD TENANT IMPROVEMENT ALLOWANCE: An allowance for items that may be installed in the leased premises of an office building at no extra charge to the tenant.

STATEMENT OF DISBURSEMENTS: The primary record produced by the management firm's accounting department for the owner; a statement of money received and money paid out.

STUDIO APARTMENT: A commonly used term to describe an efficiency or bedroom-less apartment. In certain areas, the term refers to a small apartment with two levels.

SUBDIVISION: A tract of land divided by the owner into blocks, building lots, and streets by a recorded subdivision plot; compliance with local regulations is required.

SUBLETTING: The leasing of premises by a tenant to a third party for part of the tenant's remaining term.

SUMMARY OF OPERATIONS: A brief description of income and expenses relative to a property for a specific period, usually one month.

TAX: A government levy usually made on a regular basis and based in principle on the relative value of the object being levied.

TAXABLE INCOME: Income for a given period of time against which there is an income tax liability to a municipal, provincial or federal income tax agency.

TECHNICAL OVERSUPPLY: A condition arising when there are more property units in a given community than there are consumers for them.

TENANT: One who pays rent to occupy or gain possession of real estate.

TENANCY AGREEMENT: Any agreement, usually in writing, between a landlord and another, permitting the use of property by the other under specific terms, such as use, term of occupancy, or rent.

TENANCY AT SUFFERANCE: The tenancy of a tenant who lawfully comes into possession of the landlord's real estate, but continues to occupy the premises improperly after the tenant's lease rights have expired.

TENANCY AT WILL: An estate that gives the tenant the right to possession until terminated by notice or death of the landlord. The term of this holding is indefinite.

TENANCY IN COMMON: A form of co-ownership by which each owner holds his undivided interest as though they were the sole owner; each owner has the right to partition.

TENANT MIX: The wide representation of businesses and services that comprise a shopping centre or office building; of households that comprise a multifamily development.

TERM LEASE: A binding landlord/tenant agreement for a specified time.

TITLE: The evidence of right that a person has to the ownership and possession of land.

TOWNHOUSE: A type of single-family home built as attached or semi-detached row houses.

TRAFFIC REPORT: A record of the factors that lead prospects to visit or make inquiries at a property.

TURNOVER: The number of units that are vacated during a specific period of time, usually one year. Turnover is usually expressed as a ratio between the number of units vacated and the total number of units in a particular property.

UNIT: A single, distinct part of the whole, e.g. a single apartment.

UNIT DEED: A document that legally transfers the title of a condominium unit and its undivided portion of the common areas to the owner.

UNIT MAKE-READY REPORT: A maintenance checklist for defects in a newly vacated unit.

UNIT SIZE: A listing of the number of bedrooms and baths an apartment contains.

URBAN RENEWAL: A complete program for clearing slum areas and designing redevelopment projects.

USABLE AREA: The total interior area of a particular unit or space, including partitions, which is used exclusively by a tenant.

USE CLAUSE: A provision in a lease that explicitly states how the leased area will be used.

UTILITY: A public service, such as gas, water, or electricity.

VACANCY: An area in a building that is unoccupied and available for rent.

VALUE: The worth or usefulness of a good or service expressed in terms of a specific sum of money.

VENDEE: One who purchases; the person to whom something is sold.

VENDOR: One who sells something to another.

VOID: Null, having no legal force or binding effect.

WALK-UP: An apartment building of two or more floors where the only access to the upper floors is by means of stairways.

ZONING: Any restriction on the use of real property within a given area.

JOIN US FOR
AN UPCOMING INVESTOR MEETING
FREE OF CHARGE!

- Looking to take the next step in your real estate investing career?
- Having a hard time putting together your team of professionals?
- Stuck in a rut and don't know how to get out?
- Losing money on your rentals?
- Can't find the time to locate properties that make sense?

Then let CANREIG help you!

The Canadian Real Estate Investment Group, (CANREIG), founded by an innovative investor, Dave Ravindra, who saw the need to bring viable real estate investing information to Canadian investors, has been creating millionaires for over 10 years. CANREIG's mission statement, "To create more millionaires in Canada via real estate investing above and beyond any other real estate investment company" is no small feat. By educating their members on how to make wise, creative and sound investments, this company's techniques have proven successful time and time again. Starting from small modest roots of one office in Ontario, CANREIG has grown into an international company. With offices in Vancouver, Edmonton, Calgary, Ottawa, Toronto, Montreal, Florida, and Brazil, CANREIG offers its members multi-faceted resources that enable them to make smart investment decisions. Whether real estate investing is new or familiar this company has something to offer everyone with an interest in real estate investing.

Let CANREIG help you take the next step in reaching your real estate goals!

Meetings Held Across Canada Monthly!

Call 1-866-959-0063 or email us at admin@canreig.com with reference to the code below to attend an upcoming meeting in your area for free.

CODE: PMPUB09

Note: This code cannot be used towards seminars, workshops, publications or any other CANREIG product or service except for the Investor Meeting offered by CANREIG. CANREIG reserves the right to cancel this promotion at any time without prior notice. When making reservations, please inform the representative that you have purchased this book and present it when you attend. This offer cannot be combined with any other discount, including advanced online reservation discounts. This coupon is not redeemable for cash. This coupon is non-transferable. Limit one free admittance to an Investor Meeting per person, per year. NO CASH VALUE.

Visit CANREIG at www.CANREIG.com to see how your needs can be met with professionals that understand the real estate game.